SAT SMART:

STRATEGIES AND ANSWERS TO THE SAT

By Susan Alaimo

Copyright © 2014 by SAT Smart LLC

All rights reserved.

SAT is a registered trademark of the College Board which was not involved in the production of, and does not endorse, this book. *The Official SAT Study Guide* is likewise a trademark owned by the College Board, and has no affiliation with this book. PSAT/NMSQT is a trademark jointly owned by the College Board and the National Merit Scholarship Corporation. Other products and services may be trademarks of their respective owners. None of the trademark holders are affiliated with SAT Smart or its website.

Every effort has been made to ensure that the information in this book is correct, but any use of this book or reliance on the ideas contained herein is strictly at your own risk.

Visit our website: **www.SATsmart.com**

ISBN-13: 978-0615996813
ISBN-10: 0615996817

INTRODUCTION

The purpose of *SAT SMART: STRATEGIES AND ANSWERS TO THE SAT* is to offer students the information they need to reach their potential on the all-important SAT exam. This book is focused on the current SAT exam, which is in use throughout 2014 and 2015. This book is separated into two parts: Part I provides general information on PSAT/SAT preparation, the college search process, college applications and scholarships. It also provides pointers for the college application essay.

Part II focuses on SAT preparation. It offers "SAT Smart Strategies," which teach the best techniques to tackle the Critical Reading and Math sections, as well as the ideal way to format the essay portion of the SAT exam. This is followed by detailed answers to two full-length SAT exams. Using these strategies and techniques, students should take the first two exams in *The Official SAT Study Guide* by College Board. They can certainly work on one section at a time. There is no need to complete the entire exam in one sitting. Then, they should use this guide to review their answers and note the reasoning behind each answer. This will best prepare students to get the answers correct when they see the same type of questions on the actual SAT exam. This book concludes with a guide to vocabulary preparation in the form of "300 Words Frequently Seen on the SAT."

TABLE OF CONTENTS

PART I

WHAT YOU NEED TO KNOW:

PSAT/SAT TEST PREPARATION   5

THE COLLEGE SEARCH PROCESS   9

COLLEGE APPLICATIONS   11

THE COLLEGE APPLICATION ESSAY   14

POINTERS   17

SCHOLARSHIPS   18

PART II

SAT SMART STRATEGIES   19

CRITICAL READING   20

MATH   21

ESSAY   22

MULTIPLE-CHOICE WRITING QUESTIONS   23

SCORING   23

PRACTICE, PRACTICE & THEN PRACTICE
SOME MORE!   24

SAT TEST I ANSWERS   25

SAT TEST 2 ANSWERS   69

300 WORDS FREQUENTLY SEEN ON THE SAT   114

PART I

WHAT YOU NEED TO KNOW

As you prepare to sit for the PSAT/SAT exams and to embark upon your college search, college application, and scholarship hunt journey, there is some very important information you need to know to help you have a truly successful outcome!

PSAT/SAT TEST PREPARATION

The first significant test in this process is the PSAT, which is administered each year in October. Students generally take this test in their own high schools. Many students first take the PSAT as freshmen or sophomores, but this is strictly for practice. The PSAT that "counts" is the one taken as high school juniors. Another name for the junior year PSAT is the "National Merit Scholarship Qualifying Exam," often abbreviated as the "NMSQE." This test determines which students will be named National Merit Finalists, National Merit Semi-Finalists, and National Merit Commended Students. These honors are frequently rewarded with college scholarship money. But for most students, the PSAT serves as an indication of how they should expect to score on the SAT.

The PSAT is scored in two-digit numbers. Students receive three scores: one for Math, one for Critical Reading, and one for Writing. Each score is in the 20 to 80 point range. The PSAT, like the SAT to follow, is marked on a curve, with students competing against one another. The median score for each area is approximately 50, with roughly half of all college-bound students scoring below that figure and roughly half scoring above that figure. When students are scored on the SAT, they again get three scores: one in each of the areas of Math, Critical Reading and Writing. But SAT scores range from 200 to 800 points. If students take their PSAT scores and add a zero to the end of each score, they will have a good indication of how they will score on the SAT without any further test preparation. In other words, a Math score of 54 on the PSAT will likely result in a score of about 540 on the SAT. A Critical Reading score of 63 on the PSAT will likely result in a score of about 630 on the SAT.

There is no definitive score that students need to reach to gain acceptance to a particular college. However, most colleges provide a range of scores achieved by the majority of their accepted students. The College of New Jersey, for example, which is a highly respected public university, reports its median SAT ranges as: Critical Reading 550-650 and Math 580-680. Rider University, a private university in New Jersey, reports its median SAT scores as: Critical Reading 523 and Math as 534.

Students tend to add their three scores together, focusing on their "combined score" on the SAT. However, colleges look at the three scores separately, placing much greater emphasis on the Math and Critical Reading scores. Many colleges do not even ask about the Writing score. In fact, until 2005, the PSAT and SAT exams were comprised only of Math and Critical Reading (then called Verbal) sections. Then, in March of 2005, Writing was added to the PSAT and SAT exams. One reason for this addition was that the University of California had threatened to drop the SAT as an admission requirement if the College Board did not update the test.

Students often wonder why the SAT is so important. The reason is that college admissions officers are seeking a level playing field on which to compare students from all different educational backgrounds. Within any one school, there is usually a significant difference among the grading policies of the various teachers. Some teachers are more stringent graders, while others have more relaxed grading policies. If we consider the varied educational experiences of students throughout our country, and throughout the world, these differences become even more dramatic. How does a college admissions officer compare, for example, a "B" in Geometry from a student in a large public school in North Dakota with that of a home-schooled student in Vermont or that of a private prep-school student in Arizona or that of a student in a small parochial school in Connecticut? The honest answer is that it is virtually impossible. Therefore, colleges utilize standardized tests, such as the SAT I Reasoning Test (the real name for the SAT), in order to compare applicants.

Colleges frequently use the SAT scores of their applicants as a basis for offering college scholarship (grant) money. Many colleges utilize a chart, cross-referencing a high school student's grade-point average (G.P.A.) with his or her SAT score, in order to determine the amount of scholarship money to offer. The amount of money that is offered for a student's freshman year in college is usually the basis for the amount that will be given for each of the subsequent three years. Therefore, it makes good financial sense for students to put in the time and effort necessary to earn the highest SAT score of which they are capable.

The SAT is offered several times a year, with testing dates in October, November, December, January, March, May and June. Typically, high school students take the PSAT in October of their junior year, take the SAT for the first time in January or March of their junior year, and then follow up by taking the SAT again in May or June of their junior year. If necessary, they can certainly take the test again in the fall of their senior year. It's important to know that students can take the SAT as many times as they choose. When it comes time to fill out college applications, students should go online to www.CollegeBoard.org and indicate which scores should be sent to colleges. Generally, students should send only their highest scores. Frequently, students ask whether they can send their highest Math score from one SAT test along with their highest Critical Reading score from a different SAT test. The answer to this question is that it depends on the college.

Many colleges allow students to send their highest scores from different SAT tests. This is called "super-scoring." Other colleges consider the highest combined score from one individual SAT test.

Since the SAT is so important in determining not only a student's college acceptances but also a student's scholarship offers, it is vital to be well prepared. Remember, the SAT is marked on a curve, so students are scored against their peers, many of whom will take their test preparation quite seriously! The best way to prepare for the SAT is by using the book published by College Board, *The Official SAT Study Guide*. The book includes ten practice SAT exams that reflect the exact type of material found on the actual test. The directions for each test section are, word for word, the directions on the actual test. Students should make sure they know the directions for each section in advance of taking the real test. They will therefore save time on each section – time that can be used on the actual test material. Likewise, the example question for each test section is the exact same example question for each test section on the actual test. The box of Math formulas at the beginning of each Math section on the practice tests is identical to the box of Math formulas that will be found at the beginning of each Math section on the actual test.

Since the College Board owns, publishes, and develops the SAT, it is most productive to use the College Board guide in order to prepare. (If you were trying to get your Maytag dishwasher to operate in the most efficient manner, would you use a Maytag manual or one put out by a competitor?) However, the College Board only includes an answer sheet at the end of each test, enumerating "what" the correct answers are, but not "why." Therefore, included in this book are the answers (with explanations) to each question on the first two full-length SAT exams in *The Official SAT Study Guide* by College Board (2nd edition). This is the ideal way to prepare for the actual SAT, since it introduces students to the exact type of material that they will face on the day of the real test. By reviewing the explanations in this book, students will be prepared to answer similar questions with accuracy. Also included in this book is a section on the strategies of the test, as it is vital for students to know all of the "secrets" of the SAT and feel in control, so they will go into the test with confidence and maximize their opportunity to fully reach their potential.

When questioned about their insecurities on the SAT exam, many students expressed the fear that their vocabulary is weak and will affect their success on the Critical Reading sections. To address this concern, we have included in this book a list of "300 Words Frequently Seen on the SAT" along with their definitions. (The list includes such SAT favorites as "pragmatic," "ephemeral" and "loquacious.") Students should go through this list, noting which words they already know. The remaining words, which are unfamiliar, may be made into good old-fashioned "flashcards." If students learn five new words per day, before long they will be ready to face the Critical Reading sections with confidence!

THE COLLEGE SEARCH

Searching for the ideal college can be overwhelming, but it should be great fun as well. The best place to start is on the website www.CollegeBoard.org. On this site, you can use different filters to help you narrow down your list of potential colleges from the 3,961 that are included on this website! If you first select "Type of School," and choose "4-year college or university," the list is immediately reduced to 2,297 results (eliminating 1,664 colleges!) Next, you may want to choose "Location," and either list the states in which you would consider attending college, or put in your zip code and list the geographical range in which you would consider attending college. For me, indicating that I want to attend a college within 200 miles of my zip code narrowed down my choices to 410 colleges (eliminating another 1,887 colleges)! A very important category to consider is "Major & Learning Environment." If you know the field in which you hope to major in college, you will be able to substantially narrow down your list of potential colleges. Discuss the list of colleges that you create with your college counselor, who may be able to shed light on these colleges and offer further insights from his/her vast wealth of experience.

Once you have narrowed down a potential list of "good fit" colleges, collect as much information as you can about each of these schools. A great deal of information can be gathered from the colleges' individual websites. Another great source of information is the U.S. News & World Report annual guidebook, *Best Colleges,* which is available in bookstores, supermarkets, and convenience stores, as well as online. This guidebook is so highly regarded that it is often mentioned on national evening newscasts on the day it is first released. The news angle is frequently the competition between Harvard University and Princeton University over which school garnered first place and which was relegated to second place in the U.S. News & World Report rankings. (Princeton earned top honors in 2014!) But the best use of this guide for most students is to analyze the data, for any potential college, in areas such as acceptance rate, average freshman retention rate, percent of classes under 20 students, percent of classes with 50+ students, etc.

Once a well-thought-out list of potential colleges has been developed, it's time for a road trip! Unfortunately, the best time for such a trip is NOT during summer vacation. High school students need to be able to visualize what their college experience would be like at each particular college. For this reason, it's best to visit when classes are in session, on a regular school day. During each visit, students should aim to get a feel for the atmosphere, a sense of the "typical student," a look at a "lived-in" dorm room, and a taste of the cafeteria food. At the end of each visit, students will typically have a sense of whether or not they would "fit in" and whether or not they plan to apply to that particular college. By the way, be sure to sign in at the Admissions Office of any college that you visit. Colleges keep track of who visited and when and may take that into consideration in the admission process as a sign of interest in their school.

COLLEGE APPLICATIONS

Once a student has taken the SAT for the last time and a list of "good fit" colleges has been finalized, it's time to start the college application process. This need not be a horrendous or unbearable experience. The key is to take it one step at a time. A college application typically consists of:

1) Factual information (Name, address, phone number, parents' college and employment information, etc.)
2) SAT scores
3) List of volunteer work, extracurricular activities, and work experience
4) Personal essay
5) Transcript
6) Letters of recommendation

There are two types of college applications. One is the "Common Application," which is an application that is accepted by more than 500 colleges nationwide and can only be completed online. Once students complete the Common Application, they insert the college code of each of the colleges to which they want to apply and send the application off to all of these colleges. Obviously, this is the simplest way of applying to college. The downfall is that there is no way to personalize the application. The essay that is "cut and pasted" into the Common Application is the same one that will be seen by all colleges.

The alternative way to apply to colleges is to fill out a separate application for each college (when available). Not all colleges offer students the option of filling out an application specific to their school. But when they do, the rewards can be worth the extra effort. When filling out an application for one particular college, a student can personalize the application towards that college. This is particularly feasible in the essay portion of the application, where the student can include information as to why that specific college would be a perfect match for his/her academic and career interests and talents.

When students are applying to colleges, they naturally worry about whether the colleges will accept them. The truth is, the colleges are likewise worrying about whether the students will accept them! Students today typically apply to eight or more colleges; they will only attend one. Colleges have budgets to meet totaling in the millions of dollars. They cannot accept eight times the number of students they need to meet their budget, figuring that only one in eight will likely attend. What would they do if all of the students accepted? But they obviously need to meet their enrollment requirements. So college admissions officers try to figure out which students, if accepted, would be likely to attend their college. It is therefore a great advantage to let college admissions officers know what you specifically like about their college and why you would attend, if accepted. If a college is your first choice school, be sure to let them know!

Your SAT scores are important criteria in the college application process. Some colleges allow your scores to be printed on your official high school transcript. Other colleges require that an official score report be sent to them by the College Board. Either way, be sure that you only submit your highest SAT scores!

Another significant component of the college application is the "activities" section. This is the area where students list all of their extracurricular activities, volunteer work, and job experiences. If completing the Common Application, students are required to fill in the information online. If completing an application for a specific college, it is advisable to write "see attached resume" and then include a polished resume where you can present, in decreasing order of importance, the activities in which you have been engaged during your high school years.

Note that colleges are often not looking for a Renaissance man (or woman). Rather, colleges often seek young people with a passion or specific talent that they would be bringing with them to their college campus. So students should not spread themselves too thin by participating in a multitude of activities. Colleges are much more impressed by students who are committed to achieving specific goals, such as earning a black belt in karate, Eagle Scout or Gold Award in boy or girl scouting, or becoming a varsity captain in a sport, or a student government leader.

Recommendation letters are likewise a key factor of college applications. Students should request a recommendation letter, in person, from two teachers with whom they have worked during either their junior or senior years of high school. If a teacher agrees to write a recommendation letter, the student should give the teacher a letter stating specifically what the teacher is being asked to do. Let the teacher know whether to turn in the recommendation letter to the guidance office or mail it directly to the colleges, in which case the student should supply stamped, addressed envelopes. Also, in the letter, give the teacher some factual information that could be included in the recommendation. Remind the teacher of the classes you took with him or her, your accomplishments in the class of which you are proudest, what outside activities you are involved with, etc. In other words, help the teacher by providing specific information that could be included in the recommendation. Also, allow plenty of time for the teacher to write your letter. It is disrespectful and inconsiderate to assume that a teacher will do this in a few days, or even within a week. After your applications have been submitted, be sure to thank the teachers who wrote on your behalf. Later, keep them posted of your acceptances!

As for your official transcript, be sure to follow the protocol at your high school to be sure that your transcripts are sent in a timely manner to all the colleges to which you are applying. It is extremely important in the college application process to be aware of deadlines. Colleges often have several deadlines for applications. Some colleges offer "rolling admission." This means that applications are reviewed, and decided upon, as they arrive. Students often get a decision within a few weeks after submitting their application. Another type of deadline is "early action." Early action deadlines are usually either November 1st or November 15th. If a student submits an application by this date, and indicates that he/she wants to be considered early action, then the student will get a decision in a relatively short period of time, typically between December 15th and January 15th. A student can apply early action to as many colleges as he or she chooses, and does not have to make a decision until May 1st.

Another type of deadline is "early decision." A student is allowed to submit only one early decision application and commits to attend that particular college, if accepted. The deadline for early decision applications is also typically November 1st or November 15th, and students usually get a response by December 15th. Students should only apply early decision when they are 100% sure that it is the ideal college for them!

THE COLLEGE APPLICATION ESSAY

The Common Application, which is accepted by more than 500 colleges, requires one essay that must be between 250 and 650 words. Students have a choice of five essay topics, which are listed below:

(1) "Some students have a background or story that is so central to their identity that they believe their application would be incomplete without it. If this sounds like you, then please

share your story."

This question appears to give you a great deal of freedom to write about almost anything. But do not overlook the phrase "application would be incomplete without it." They do not want a recap of your activities, school grades, or impressive SAT scores. They also do not want a story that hundreds of applicants could tell. The essay needs to be key to your identity. Do you have a particular passion that has been an integral part of your life for many years? Are there challenges in your home life that have placed great responsibilities on you over the years? Did you, or someone close to you, have significant challenges to overcome that have greatly impacted your life? The story you tell here needs to be central to your identity: one that your application would have been incomplete without!

(2) "Recount an incident or time when you experienced failure. How did it affect you, and what lessons did you learn?"

The key to this essay topic is to show that you were able to successfully face a failure, learn from it, and show substantial inner growth. At the start of the essay you need to "recount" – give the plot summary – of the failure that you experienced. An important part of this essay is your account of how the "failure" affected you. How did you respond? What emotions did you experience? Were you shocked, disappointed, or frustrated? The last part of this essay question is key. What lessons did you learn? They are looking here for introspection and self-analysis. Did the failure motivate you? Were you able to make something positive out of a negative experience? Are you a better person today because of the failure that you faced in your past?

(3) "Reflect on a time when you challenged a belief or idea. What prompted you to act? Would you make the same decision again?"

The idea or belief that you reflect upon shouldn't be something superficial. It should be one that you care deeply about and about which you can express your passion. Your essay should depict you as a thoughtful, analytical and open-minded individual. Note the second part of the question, which asks if you would make the same decision again. If you re-evaluated and challenged your own beliefs, you demonstrate that you possess the self-awareness, open-mindedness and maturity that are desirable qualities in college students. If you hold strongly to your belief or idea and would undertake the same challenge today, then you can show yourself to be a highly ethical, principled individual who would be an asset to a college community. Just be careful before you broach a highly controversial belief or idea, particularly in the area of religion or politics. You don't want to alienate the admissions counselor!

(4) "Describe a place or environment where you are perfectly content. What do you do or experience there, and why is it meaningful to you?"

A place or environment could be almost anywhere. Think about where and when you are most content, and analyze the source of that feeling of contentment. Elaborate on the time that you spend in this environment. Keep in mind the importance of the "why is it meaningful to you" portion of the question. You are being asked by the admissions officers to be introspective and share what it is that you value.

(5) "Discuss an accomplishment or event, formal or informal, that marked your transition from childhood to adulthood within your culture, community, or family."

This prompt allows you to explore a single event or achievement that marked a clear milestone in your personal development. As with the other topics, the admissions officers are looking for a sense of introspection and self-analysis. The event that you choose to write about should be one that had a significant, long term effect. Perhaps it's one that allowed you to experience a new sense of maturity and responsibility. Be careful to avoid the "hero" essay: the one about scoring the winning touchdown, being chosen prom king or queen, or other scenario in which you were the star of the day. They are looking for an event from which you gleaned great insight into the qualities that you hope to possess or goals that you aspire to achieve.

POINTERS

Realize that the essay is the one portion of your application that you can personalize. This is your opportunity to tell the college admissions officers whatever you want them to know about you. Think about your qualities, accomplishments, passions, and anything else that is not reflected in the other parts of your application. Make the most of this opportunity to let admissions officers get to know what an awesome person you are!

Know that your Common Application Essay is "locked" and cannot be personalized for each individual college application. So if, for instance, you plan first to send your Common Application to Villanova University and you mention in your essay that Villanova would be the ideal college for your academic interests, every subsequent college to which you send the Common Application will get the essay stating that you want to attend Villanova! The only way to personalize your college essay to a specific college is to use that college's individual application rather than the Common Application.

Brainstorm: What are some of your favorite memories? Why are they important to you? What do they say about you? Have you ever experienced something that stopped you in your tracks? Let your essay convey a sense of who you are -- something not conveyed by your transcript, SAT scores, or list of activities. Don't write about what you think the college admissions people want to hear. Write about something you really feel strongly about. Your passion and personality will shine through.

Be positive, not negative. Never place blame on other people. Do not write about a teacher who did not understand you or a coach who did not recognize your talents. It is certainly acceptable to write about a failure that you experienced (which is the topic of Essay #2) as long as you show what you learned from the experience and how, in the end, you benefitted from the experience.

Recognize that almost anything you want to write about can be tweaked to fit one of the five Common Application essay topics. Often it is easiest to write the body of your essay first. Then write your introduction, foreshadowing what you will share in the body of your essay and tailoring the introduction to specifically address one of the five essay topics. Be sure to write a solid conclusion. If appropriate, this is a great place to share your hopes and dreams for your upcoming college education.

SCHOLARSHIPS

Once students are accepted to college, they frequently seek scholarship money. There are two types of funds that are awarded to students. Merit awards are based on academic achievement and are usually called "grants." They do not get paid back. In other words, this is scholarship money. Need-based aid is awarded based on the financial needs of the student and his/her parents. In order to be considered for need-based aid, parents must file a FAFSA (Free Application for Federal Student Aid) after January 1st of the student's senior year. Some colleges have additional requirements in order to apply for need-based aid. A popular form required by many colleges is the College Scholarship Service (CSS) PROFILE. Be sure to be in contact with the Financial Aid Office of any college that you may attend, asking about any scholarships for which you could apply and any forms that would need to be submitted.

Most scholarships originate at the college level. There are also many national scholarships offered by such companies as Coca-Cola, Toyota, Pepsi-Co and Discover. But the likelihood of being awarded scholarship money in a national competition is minimal. The best source for scholarship money, outside of the college you will be attending, is within your local community. High school guidance offices collect information on scholarships offered by groups within your community, such as the Rotary and Kiwanis Clubs. Also, contact any group of which either you or your parents are members to inquire about potential scholarships. These include the employers of both you and your parents, churches, temples, Girl Scouts, Boy Scouts, Knights of Columbus, The 4-H Club, etc.

PART II

SAT SMART STRATEGIES

There are three areas of the SAT -- Critical Reading, Math and Writing -- with three sections for each area. Students get a separate score for each area, ranging between 200 and 800. The SAT is marked on a curve, so students are actually scored against each other. A score of 500 is approximately the median score for each area, with a score of 600 giving students many more college and scholarship options. Students can take the SAT as many times as they like. It is offered each year in September, October, November, December, January, March, May and June. Once they have finished taking the SAT for the last time, students go to the website, www.CollegeBoard.org, and pick which scores (the highest!) they want sent to the colleges to which they are applying. Some colleges allow students to "super-score," which is to send their highest Math score from one exam and their highest Critical Reading score from another. Most colleges are not too concerned about the Writing score and use it simply to place students in their freshman year writing class.

Students typically start the SAT process by taking the PSAT in October of their junior year. (Some students take the PSAT as sophomores, and even as freshmen, but these scores serve no official purpose until their junior year.) The PSAT is simply a shortened version of the SAT, with the same type of questions and the same level of difficulty. If a student has prepared for the PSAT, then it is a good indication of how the student should expect to score on the SAT. Another name for the PSAT is the NMSQE (National Merit Scholarship Qualifying Exam) because it identifies National Merit Scholars and awards scholarship money.

For a student to maximize his or her potential on the SAT, it is extremely beneficial to be aware of the strategies for each test section:

Critical Reading

The Critical Reading area of the SAT is the one most students dread, as they typically read through long, tedious passages, realizing at the end that their minds have wandered and they are not at all sure about what they have read. Should they read the passage again, or, since time is ticking by, go right to the questions and hope for the best?

The secret behind the Critical Reading questions is that they go in order, not from easy to hard (as is typical on all other SAT sections), but in the order in which the information is presented in the passage. So, a student should first read the introductory material, which puts the passage into context, and then read the passage one paragraph at a time, answering the questions as he or she moves through the passage. Most questions on these sections state the lines that should be referred to in order to answer the questions. So, if the first question references lines 7 to 9, for example, a student should read through to the end of the paragraph that contains those lines, and then answer that question. If the next question references lines 19 to 21, the student should continue reading the passage until the end of the paragraph containing those particular lines. This is the pattern to use throughout the passage. Typically, the last few questions are overall questions, based on the passage as a whole. Occasionally, one or two of these overall questions are placed at the beginning of the series of questions; students should simply skip them and return to them after having read the entire passage.

The Critical Reading sections also contain Sentence Completions. These are sentences with one or two blanks and five choices of words or pairs of words from which a student must select the best option to fill in the blanks. The first few sentences are typically straightforward with vocabulary words familiar to most students. The last few sentences usually contain vocabulary words that are unfamiliar to most students. There are a few strategies that can be utilized here. First of all, when a student is reading a sentence, he or she should fill in the blanks with words that come to mind, without looking at the multiple-choice options. Then, even if the "created" words are not offered, ones with a similar meaning should be. Also, when a student is not sure of a word's meaning, he or she should think of the context in which the word is used. For example, many students cannot define "murky." But when asked what gets "murky," many students respond with the word "water." What does murky water look like? Students know that it is dirty, or lacks clarity, and that is usually sufficient to choose the correct answer.

MATH

It is important for students to know that the Math questions on each SAT section go in order from easy to hard. The first, easy question counts just as much as the last, hard question.

So a student should not race through the earlier, easy questions (and possibly make careless mistakes) just to get to the last few, strenuous questions that are designed to elude most students. Students should remember that a box with geometric formulas will always appear at the beginning of each Math section. So students do not need to memorize the formulas for the area of a circle, volume of a cylinder, and so on. Also, students are allowed to bring, and use, a calculator -- even a graphing calculator! And students are allowed to write in their test booklet, using it as scrap paper.

All Math questions are multiple-choice, with the exception of ten open-ended (grid-in) questions. These appear in the section with 18 questions, with multiple-choice questions 1 through 8 ranging from easy to hard and open-ended questions 9 to 18 ranging from easy to hard. The open-ended questions are the only questions on the SAT where wrong answers do not incur a penalty. Since they are not multiple-choice, the chance of randomly guessing the correct answer is minimal in the eyes of test-makers. But you have nothing to lose, so go ahead and take a good guess!

ESSAY

The first section of the SAT is always a 25-minute timed writing exercise, known as the Essay. Two readers score each essay on a scale from 0 to 6, and these scores are added together. The key to getting a high score on the essay is to know the rubric on which it is scored and to write accordingly. The strategy is to be sure to stick to the topic and to follow the outline below:

Paragraph 1: Write your thesis statement.
            (Answer the question directly.)
            State two to three examples on which you will
            elaborate to support your thesis statement.
Paragraph 2: Elaborate on your first example.
Paragraph 3: Elaborate on your second example.

Paragraph 4: This paragraph is optional. If you introduced a third example, then elaborate on it in this paragraph.

Conclusion: Restate your thesis statement and the main points of your examples.

MULTIPLE-CHOICE WRITING QUESTIONS

While the essay counts as 30 percent of the writing score, the 49 multiple-choice writing questions, which are divided between two sections, determine 70 percent of the student's writing score. These questions are based on identifying grammatical errors, such as agreement of tense, use of the proper pronoun, parallel sentence structure, and agreement of subject and verb. By reviewing the most common grammatical rules learned in their earlier years of education, many students can quickly master these sections. These rules are also reviewed in Part III of *The Official SAT Study Guide* by College Board.

parallelism   *Verb/tense*   *Subj/A.O.*
sing/Pl

SCORING

The SAT is marked on a curve, with each student awarded a score ranging between 200 and 800 on each area: Critical Reading, Math and Writing. With the exception of ten "open-ended" Math questions and the essay, all questions are multiple-choice. Regarding these multiple-choice questions, students are awarded one point for each correct answer, and deducted 1/4 point for each incorrect answer. Questions left blank do not earn or lose points. So, for example, if a student gets 40 of the Math questions correct (out of the 54 on each SAT exam), he or she will be awarded 40 points. If that same student got 8 questions wrong, then 2 points would be deducted from those points, leaving the student with 38 points. (The 6 answers left blank would not add or deduct points from the student's score.) Using a "Conversion Table," students would find that a score of 38 points in Math would result in a score of approximately 610. Scoring is completed in the same way for Critical Reading.

The Writing score is figured in a different manner. Students are awarded a score ranging between 0 and 12 for their essay. This determines about 30% of the Writing score. The balance of the score (about 70%) is based on the 49 multiple-choice questions that are divided between two Writing sections on the SAT. Students earn one point for each correct answer and lose 1/4 point for each incorrect answer. Once again, blank answers do not earn or lose points. There is a "Conversion Table" where the essay score and "multiple-choice raw score" are cross-referenced to produce an SAT Writing score. When completing practice tests in *The Official SAT Study Guide* by College Board, students will find a Conversion Table for each area at the end of each test.

PRACTICE, PRACTICE, AND THEN PRACTICE SOME MORE!

The format and content of the SAT is not a secret. In fact any student can purchase a book with ten full-length SAT exams, written by the College Board, with directions, sample questions, and a box of Math formulas that is identical, word for word, to what appears on every SAT exam. The content of each section likewise mirrors what a student will find on his or her SAT exam. The strategy of mastering the SAT is therefore the same one used to achieve success in any area of life, whether attempting to become a professional athlete, a celebrated musician, or a gourmet chef: practice, practice, and then practice some more!

Since you now have a good understanding of the best strategies for the SAT, the next, and most important, step is to practice. The section that follows provides detailed answers to the questions on the first two full-length exams in *The Official SAT Study Guide* by College Board. The reason this is of immense help is that *The Official SAT Study Guide* provides an answer key at the end of each test that simply indicates what the correct answers are, but not how to get them. It is not enough simply to complete practice exams. The key to improving your score is to find out why you got certain questions wrong and to learn from your mistakes! Otherwise, you will simply repeat the same errors on the "real" test. Didn't Albert Einstein define "insanity" as doing the same thing over and over again and expecting different results?

With that in mind, get to work on the first two tests in *The Official SAT Study Guide.* Work on one section at a time, carefully checking your work with the correct answers detailed in this book. Over time, review the last portion of this book, featuring "300 Words Frequently Seen on the SAT." If you review ten words per day, you will master, in a month, some vocabulary that might otherwise cause you great stress on the day of your big test!

Test 1

Section 2: Critical Reading

Question: 1
Answer: A

> Vocabulary:
> A) **foresight (anticipation)**
> B) nostalgia (homesickness)
> C) folly (recklessness, foolishness)
> D) despair (hopelessness, misery)
> E) artistry (originality, creativity)

The Russian writer "accurately predicted" what would happen. He therefore had foresight, which means to have a sense, in advance, of something that is going to happen.

Question: 2
Answer: B

Vocabulary:
A) intricate (complicated)
B) candid (straightforward)
C) ostentatious (showy, pretentious)
D) fictional (imaginary)
E) convoluted (elaborate)

Since the images are "simple and direct," they provide an honest, straightforward reflection which can best be characterized as candid.

Question: 3
Answer: A

Vocabulary:
A) **capricious (unpredictable, erratic)**
B) bombastic (pretentious, overbearing)
C) loquacious (talkative)
D) dispassionate (without passion or feeling)
E) decorous (well-mannered, proper)

Since Kate acted in an unpredictable and erratic manner, her friends would consider her to be capricious.

Question: 4
Answer: D

Vocabulary:
A) an emotional (expressive, sensitive) intellectual (knowledgeable)
B) a chance (accidental, coincidental) random (unplanned, unintentional)
C) an intuitive (innate, instinctive) impulsive (thoughtless, impetuous)
D) a deliberate (thoughtful) instinctive (natural, innate)
E) an intentional (deliberate, purposeful) logical (common-sense)

In this sentence we have two comparisons. A decision was "visceral" (or instinctual) rather than _____. Here we need a word that means well thought out. And is was not "rational" (or logical) but _____. Here we need a word that means not thought out, but acting on instinct.

Question: 5
Answer: C

> Vocabulary:
> A) streamlined (modernized, efficient) infighting (bickering, squabbling)
> B) mitigated (alleviated or lessened, diminished) jingoism (chauvinism or patriotism)
> **C) ossified (solidified, hardened) bureaucratization (to complicate with a lot of rules)**
> D) politicized (to raise awareness, debate) innovation (novelty, invention)
> E) venerable (worshipped, greatly respected) legislation (law-making)

By losing versatility and adaptability, the creative business ideas became ossified or hardened. Their "transformation into rigid policies" is pretty much the definition of bureaucratization.

Question: 6
Answer: D

In the sentence before, "it felt good to be human," the author mentioned that the wild horses never "glanced skyward." They missed the "wondrous spectacle" of the night sky, clearly not appreciating nature's beauty.

Question: 7
Answer: B

"Feathery fishing lure" and "stars winked" are examples of metaphorical language. A metaphor is a comparison that doesn't use the words "like" or "as."

Question: 8
Answer: C

This paragraph is all about the reasons why Augusta Ada King is so famous. It talks about her influence on computer science, but also about the fact that she comes from a famous family.

Question: 9
Answer: A

The clue is in the middle of the paragraph when it says that "her fascinating life and lineage…she was the daughter of the flamboyant poet Lord Byron…..turned her into an icon."

Question: 10
Answer: D

The last sentence of the introduction states that, in the passage, the author "offers his views on the historical relationship between Black Americans and Black Africans." He reinforces that theme in the first sentence of the second paragraph when he states that "Black Americans have managed to sustain links with the continent of their origin…." and then elaborates on that point.

Question: 11
Answer: B

The passage states that the ancestors were sending "a clear and powerful message" and then goes on to give a warning (or advice).

Question: 12

Answer: C

The clue to the answer is in the sentence following the proverb when it states that "this maxim conveys the seemingly instinctive pull of one's heritage, our inborn curiosity in our origins...."

Question: 13
Answer: E

The contextual clues for "shadowy" come at the end of the sentence when it says that it does "not usually hold up in the light of real experience." It therefore lacks substance, or is unsubstantiated.

Question: 14
Answer: E

Line 42 starts with the words "we wondered" (which conveys doubt) and line 50 concludes with the words "the world has been forced to take note" (which conveys pride).

Question: 15
Answer: B

There are broad statements, throughout the passage, of how Black Americans and Black Africans have sought to maintain ties over the years....but nothing really specific.

Question: 16
Answer: C

The first paragraph of each of these passages focuses on the fact that the Mona Lisa is the world's most famous painting.

Question: 17
Answer: A

The author of passage 2 starts out with the question, "Why is the Mona Lisa the best-known painting in the entire world? The reasons are then elaborated in the first paragraph of passage one.

Question: 18
Answer: E

The contrast in these lines is the fact that "its subject was nobody special" but her portrait "set the standard for High Renaissance paintings."

Question: 19
Answer: B

Leonardo da Vinci described his technique as rendering his works "without lines or borders, in the manner of smoke." He is therefore characterizing an effect on his works.

Question: 20
Answer: A

The author of passage 1 ends with the sentence, "And then there's that famous smile...." which is clearly a reference to her mouth.

Question: 21
Answer: D

This is a vocabulary in context question. Which word can be substituted in for "position" in line 41? It is still the "position" (view) of many art critics.

Question: 22
Answer: E

Both the author of passage 1 and Paul Barolsky refer to the fact that there is the impression of the Mona Lisa being three dimensional. In lines 10 to 11 it states that there is "the illusion of depth." And lines 21 to 22 state "he built the illusion of three-dimensional features." Likewise, Paul Barolski, in line 56, talks about the qualities of texture and depth in the Mona Lisa.

Question: 23
Answer: E

The author put the word in quotes to show disagreement with the standard usage of the word.

Question: 24
Answer: C

Passage 1 focuses, to a great extent, on the innovative techniques used by Leonardo da Vinci in creating the Mona Lisa. Passage 2 both starts and ends with a reference to the Mona Lisa being the best-known painting in the world.

Test 1

Section 3: Math

Question: 1
Answer: A

Substitute 4 for x in each answer choice to determine which is the greatest. You will get answers 30, 15, 12, 10 and 0. Clearly, 30 is the greatest.

Question: 2
Answer: E

All of the necessary information is provided, but in a mixed up order.

The last sentence states that B = 7 mph.
The second sentence states that A = 3B, so A = 21
The end of the second sentence states that C = twice A
So C = 2 times 21 which is 42 mph

Question: 3
Answer: B

If three numbers average 8, they add up to 3 times 8, which is 24.
Therefore: x + 5x + 6x = 24
Combine like terms: 12x = 24
Divide both sides by 12
Solve that X = 2

Question: 4
Answer: D

On graphs A, B, C, and E there are several points with the same X value. Therefore, the answer is D.

Question: 5
Answer: C

The Venn diagram shows that nine students studied butterflies only. Add up all of the students to find that there is a total of 30 students.
(9 + 3 + 15 + 3)
So 9 out of 30 students studied butterflies only.
Use your calculator: 9/30 = .30 which is 30 percent

Question: 6
Answer: C

First find the length of line segment CD.
It spans from an x value -4 to an x value of 6. So CD is 10 units long.

Since line segment AB is equal to line segment CD, AB must also be 10 units long.
AB therefore spans from a y value of 3 to a y value of -7 because from 3 to -7 is a length of 10. So t = -7

Question: 7
Answer: D

Solve each one separately.
First, solve for $3x^2 = 12$
Divide both sides by 3 and find that $x^2 = 4$
Next, solve for $4y = 12$
Divide both sides by 4 and fine that $y = 3$
The question asks for the value of x^2y, so 4 times 3 equals 12.

Question: 8
Answer: D

Write the numbers right on the diagram to make it visual.
The radius of circle A is 2, so write a 2 on each side of point A in the diagram.
Next, the radius of both circle B and circle C are 4. So if the radius of each circle is 4, then the diameter of each circle is 8.
Label the diameter of circle B and circle C each 8.
Look at the diagram.
The length from point A to the circle is 2 (the radius of circle A) plus 8 (the diameter of either circle B or circle C) which equals 10.

Question: 9
Answer: D

Calculate the distance from 2 to 42. $(42 - 2 = 40)$
There are five equal spaces between 2 and 42.
So divide 40 by 5 to get 8 (the distance between any two tick marks).
The distance from 2 to x is two tick marks.

So start at 2 and add 8 to get to the first tick mark, and another 8 to get to the second tick mark, which is labeled "x"
2 + 8 + 8 = 18

Question: 10
Answer: C

Be sure to notice that x is the sum of two angles, angle SOR and angle ROV.
The easiest way to solve for x is to remember that every circle totals 360 degrees.
Put 360 in your calculator and then subtract the measure of the angles that are NOT part of x.
Therefore, 360 − 110 − 30 − 90 = 130.

Question: 11
Answer: B

If you take the divisor, which is 7, and add it to the remainder, which is 6, you will find a value for k, which is 13.
Then, answer the question by substituting 13 in for k.
The remainder when 13 + 2 is divided by 7 is 1 because 7 goes into 15 two times with 1 left over.

Question: 12
Answer: D

Note from the chart that as the depth increases, the pressure also increases. (That eliminates choices A and B)
Note that when the depth is 0, the pressure is a positive number. That makes D the only possible answer.

Question: 13
Answer: E

Write out the sequence, following the direction to multiply each number by negative 2 to get the next, sequential number.

The first term is stated to be 1. The following terms are therefore:
-2 (2nd term), 4 (3rd term), -8 (4th term), 16 (5th term), and -32 (6th term and the answer).

Question: 14
Answer: E

Foil the numbers and get $4x^2 - 25 = 5$
Add 25 to both sides and you have solved the problem:
$4x^2 = 30$.

Question: 15
Answer: B

Looking at the graph indicates that it has a negative slope. (It is heading down as it goes from left to right.)
That narrows down the choices to A (-2) or B (-1/2).
Because the absolute value of p is greater than the absolute value of r, the answer has to be B. Remember that slope is the difference in the y coordinates over the difference in the x coordinates and the line passes through origin, with coordinates (0, 0).

Question: 16
Answer: A

Subtract b from both sides of the equation.
The new equation is: $3a + 3b = 0$
Multiply both sides of the equation by 2
You now have the answer: $6a + 6b = 0$

Question: 17
Answer: C

This figure is comprised of many isosceles right triangles.
First look at the total triangle, triangle ABC.

Since F is the midpoint of side BC, it splits that segment into two congruent parts, each with length 5 square root of 2. Since line segment FC (with a length of 5 square root of 2) is the hypotenuse of the little triangle on the right, then its legs are each 5. The same is true for the little triangle on the left, as well as the top two triangles.
The shaded rectangle therefore measures 5 by 10 (length times width) giving it an area of 50.

Question: 18
Answer: D

Choose an easy pair of values and substitute them in.
The chart indicates that when x = 0, f(x) = ½
Substitute them in to find that ½ = k times a to the zero power.
Any number to the zero power is 1, so k = ½
Now substitute in another pair of values.
The chart indicates that when x = 1, f(x) = 2
So 2 = k times a to the first power.
We know that k = ½, and any number to the first power equals itself
So 2 = ½ times a
Divide both sides by ½ to find that a = 2

Question: 19
Answer: A

First, recognize that the base is a square with sides of m, so a diagonal of the base would be m times the square root of two (forming two isosceles right triangles)
Half of the diagonal would be:
m times the square root of two/2
We are told in the problem that e = m,
so rename side e to be m.
Use the Pythagorean Theorem to solve:
h squared + (m times the square root of 2/2) squared = m squared

You now have: h squared + ½ m squared =   m squared
Subtract ½ m squared from both sides
You now have h squared = m squared/2
Get the square root of both sides, and you have the answer
h = m/square root of 2

Question: 20
Answer: A

If two cars sold for $14,000 each, the total selling price would
be 2 times $14,000 which is $28,000.
A salesperson's commission is k percent of the sale.
So the answer is: k/100 (which is k percent) times $28,000
This equals 280k

Test 1

Section 5: Critical Reading

Question: 1
Answer: C

> Vocabulary:
> A) cowardice (timidity, fearfulness)
> B) prudence (cautiousness, practicality)
> **C) hospitality (friendliness, warmth, kindness)**
> D) aloofness (coldness, unfriendliness,
>   unapproachable)
> E) loyalty (faithfulness, devotion)

Someone who is welcoming is displaying the quality of
hospitality.

Question: 2
Answer: B

> Vocabulary:
> A) applauded (much admired, congratulated)

B) derailed (disrupted, ruined)
C) acknowledged (recognized, accredited)
D) permitted (allowed, accepted)
E) anticipated (expected, predicted)

If the supporters were disappointed, then the plan was side-tracked, ruined or cancelled. The correct word has to have a negative connotation, and derailed is the only negative word among the choices.

Question: 3
Answer: C

Vocabulary:
A) Condition (state, circumstance)
B) Highlight (feature, focus)
C) Stimulus (inducement, motivation)
D) Dictum (pronouncement, statement, motto)
E) Respite (break, reprieve)

Since it increases brain activity, it's used as a stimulus to help children learn.

Question: 4
Answer: A

Vocabulary:
A) negotiate (discuss, bargain) concessions (compromises, allowances)
B) antagonize (upset, alienate) friends (associates)
C) surrender (give up, admit defeat) enemies (opponents, rivals)
D) dominate (control, lead, rule) inquiries (questions, investigations)
E) equivocate (be evasive, beat around the bush) denunciations (criticisms, accusations)

The sentence says that there is a "subtle" difference, which means a slight difference. The only pair of words that will work for both blanks is choice A, since there is a slight difference between negotiating (when both sides try to get a fair deal) and conceding (when one side gives in to the other).

Question: 5
Answer: D

Vocabulary:
A) rousing (inspiring) memorable (unforgettable)
B) pedestrian (uninspired, ordinary) evolving (developing)
C) chaotic (confused, disordered) unprecedented (first time, unparalleled)
D) derivative (copied, unoriginal) inept (incompetent, clumsy)
E) spontaneous (spur of the moment, impulsive) graceless (clumsy, awkward)

The word for the first blank relates to "each move taken from another artist," so "derivative" is the only choice that fits. The word for the second blank relates to "poorly executed." Both "inept" and "graceless" would work. Since we need to choose an answer where both words work, the correct answer is D.

Question: 6
Answer: B

Vocabulary:
A) cheapened (devalued, depreciated) affordable (reasonably priced)
B) transformed (altered, changed) viable (practical, feasible)
C) revolutionized (transformed, updated) prohibitive (unaffordable, high-priced)
D) provoked (incited, aggravated) improbable (doubtful, unlikely)

E) stimulated (encouraged, inspired) inaccessible (difficult to get to)

For the first blank, "transformed" and "revolutionized" both work, narrowing down the possible answers to B and C. For the second blank, we want a word that means "affordable" or "practical." The possible answers for the second blank are therefore A and B. The only choice with acceptable answers for both blanks is therefore B.

Question: 7
Answer: D

Vocabulary:
A) cryptic (puzzling, mysterious)
B) judicious (cautious, sensible)
C) jubilant (overjoyed, triumphant)
D) supercilious (arrogant, superior)
E) pugnacious (aggressive, confrontational)

Phillip acted as though he was superior to his friends, making the correct answer "supercilious."

Question: 8
Answer: C

Vocabulary:
A) belligerence (hostility, aggression)
B) indigence (poverty)
C) perfidy (disloyalty, treachery)
D) aspersion (slander, criticism)
E) tenacity (insistence, stubbornness)

The sentence makes it very clear that we need a word that means "disloyalty," making the correct choice "perfidy" which is a synonym for disloyalty.

Question: 9

Answer: A

The teachers in Passage 1 assigned Walden as an example of "living in solitary harmony with nature" and talk about the "intrusion into pastoral harmony of the forces of industrialization." Passage 2, however, says that Walden was, at times, "downright enthusiastic" about mechanization. Therefore answer A explains just what they disagreed about.

Question: 10
Answer: B

Passage 1 talks about the "intrusion into pastoral harmony of the forces of industrialization." It therefore implies that Thoreau would view mechanization as a destructive force.

Question: 11
Answer: E

The author of Passage 1 would say that, although Thoreau may have been excited about the railroad, that is not how he usually felt about mechanization. Therefore, his enthusiasm about the railroad was "atypical," or not typical, of his usual attitude.

Question: 12
Answer: C

The author of Passage 1 would state that Passage 2 does not present Walden in the way it was perceived by generations of students who were assigned to read this book as an "illustration of the intensity with which 19th century America protested…..the forces of industrialization."

Question: 13
Answer: D

Read line 1 and think of a word that you would substitute in for "vision." Perhaps the word "view" or "idea"? Now look at the word choices and pick the word with the closest meaning, which is "conception."

Question: 14
Answer: D

In the first paragraph, the author talks about one view of the city that gets his "hackles up" – in other words, it gets him upset...he disagrees with it. The second paragraph explains the argument with which he disagrees. This question asks how the author would describe the "happier state" mentioned in the second paragraph. Since he disagrees with it, he would describe it as a "false supposition" or a false belief.

Question: 15
Answer: E

The author talks, in lines 14-19, about people who think there is a natural balance to nature. They view all that has happened since the Industrial Revolution as a "wrong turning....a blind alley." This directs us to Answer E.

Question: 16
Answer: E

The author starts the paragraph, that includes line 28, with the statement, "What bothers me about this point of view is......" Therefore, he disagrees with the views of the "thinkers." He thinks their views are wrong, which is the meaning of "erroneous." (To remember this word, notice that the beginning of the word "erroneous" looks like the word "error."

Question: 17
Answer: B

The author states, in the paragraph that contains lines 33-36, that just as ants build anthills and beavers build dams, human beings build cities. He says there is nothing unnatural about this.

Question: 18
Answer: E

The author loves cities. In the paragraph that contains line 48, the author talks about all of the positive attributes of cities, including the trash that is left around to serve as sources of food for animals. Therefore we need a positive word to describe the author's attitude, and the only positive one listed is "appreciation."

Question: 19
Answer: A

The first sentence, beginning in line 57, is the thesis statement. It is then supported by three arguments. "At the most obvious level…..." "At a somewhat deeper level….," and "Finally….." This leads us to Answer A.

Question: 20
Answer: D

Read line 63 and choose a word that you would substitute for "peculiar." Perhaps you would pick "unique"? Look at the choices and select the one that is closest in meaning, which would be "distinctive."

Question: 21
Answer: A

The author would certainly approve of the creation of a "subfield of science" in the field of Urban Ecology. He actually refers to it as the "ultimate academic accolade." An accolade in a great honor, so approval is the only possible answer.

Question: 22
Answer: C

In the paragraph that contains lines 67 to 73, the word "both" is used four times....clearly this is a comparison!

Question: 23
Answer: E

The paragraph that consists of lines 74 to 81 discusses how laws of nature (natural principles) control everything that humans can do.

Question: 24
Answer: E

The final paragraph starts with the words, "So let me state this explicitly..." (Explicitly means clearly, plainly, unequivocally). The author then repeats, or emphasizes, his main point.

Test 1

Section 6: Writing

Question: 1
Answer: C

Choice C is the only grammatically correct way of wording the sentence.

Question: 2
Answer: C

Choice C explains directly and succinctly why it's hard to determine the depths of the ocean.

Question: 3
Answer: B

Look to keep the sentence direct and simple. Several fires "were caused...."

Question: 4
Answer: C

We are looking for parallel sentence structure here. The doctor "disproved".......when she "showed." We need to use the same form of the verb.

Question: 5
Answer: E

Note that a semi-colon is used when each part of the sentence can stand alone as a grammatically correct sentence. That is what we have here. Also, the correct sentence has to show contrast, as it does here with the word "however."

Question: 6
Answer: A

This sentence requires parallel sentence structure, which it has in its current form. The three volumes...."begin with.......and culminate with." Remember that "Choice A," in this portion of the multiple choice writing section, means "no change."

Question: 7
Answer: D

The information in this sentence is best presented in a straight-forward, sequential manner.

Question: 8
Answer: A

The sentence is already in its simplest, most direct form. To be sure that the original sentence is correct grammatically, eliminate the clause between the commas and you will see that the sentence still works.

Question: 9
Answer: E

We are looking for parallel sentence construction here. The symphony was called "confusing because of....but elegant because of....."

Question: 10
Answer: C

Keep the sentence simple, direct and straightforward. There is no reason to start the sentence with the word "by," therefore eliminating choices A and B. And choices D and E are both awkward and grammatically incorrect.

Question: 11
Answer: E

If you take out the clause when you read the sentence, it is much easier to find the correct answer. Eliminate the words "as many people assume" and you notice that choice E is the direct, straightforward way of wording the sentence.

Question: 12
Answer: C

Larissa and Tariq are two different people, so they plan to become entomologists.

Question: 13
Answer: E

The entire sentence is grammatically correct, so the answer is E.

Question: 14
Answer: A

The casserole, or anything else, could smell "bad" but things cannot smell "badly."

Question: 15
Answer: C

The entire sentence is in the past tense. So choice C must be changed to read "sought out."

Question: 16
Answer: D

We are looking for parallel sentence structure here. Choice D should read "to suppress" in order to be parallel with "to display."

Question: 17
Answer: C

The average age of college students has risen quite "noticeably" not "noticeable."

Question: 18
Answer: A

Whenever you have the word "either" in a sentence, you have to have the word "or." Whenever you have the word "neither" in a sentence, you have to have the word "nor."

Question: 19
Answer: C

Since the word passengers is plural, they must purchase "their" tickets. A passenger would purchase his or her ticket.

Question: 20
Answer: E

The entire sentence is grammatically correct, so the answer is E.

Question: 21
Answer: B

You cannot compare Rockwell's paintings, to a person (Robert Rauschenberg). You have to compare people to people, or items to items.

Question: 22
Answer: E

The entire sentence is grammatically correct, so the answer is E.

Question: 23
Answer: C

The grooved and barbed spears ARE released. Always make sure that the verb agrees with the subject, even when they are not placed next to each other.

Question: 24
Answer: E

The entire sentence is grammatically correct, so the answer is E.

Question: 25
Answer: C

The problem here is word usage....it should be "of distinguishing" not "to distinguish."

Question: 26
Answer: D

The subject of the sentence is Hershey, Pennsylvania. "It's name was changed......to honor one of IT'S (not "their") famous residents."

Question: 27
Answer: E

The entire sentence is grammatically correct, so the answer is E.

Question: 28
Answer: D

"my low grades......REQUIRE (not requires) me"   Again, the subject and the verb must agree, even when not placed next to each other.

Question: 29
Answer: D

This is a comparison sentence where a story is being compared to a person. We need to replace "than baseball's" with "than that of baseball's" or "than the story of baseball's"

Question: 30

Answer: C

The introductory sentence introduces the terms "castle" and "palace." The paragraph goes on to elaborate on just what a castle is, but fails to elaborate on what a palace is.

Question: 31
Answer: C

This question calls for a linking sentence that focuses on those who put their lives in danger attempting to gain access to castles of the Middle Ages.

Question: 32
Answer: E

The simplest, most direct way of combining the information in both sentences is presented in choice E.

Question: 33
Answer: C

Sentence 9 is a statement that conveys irony. Castles that were once fortified to prevent people from entering, now "attract visitors from all over the world."

Question: 34
Answer: D

Sentence D best provides a transition between a well maintained castle and chateau, and "decaying remnants of a castle."

Question: 35
Answer: B

Basically, we are being asked for the best conclusion sentence for the passage. We do not want to introduce any new information, but rather wrap up what is being discussed in the last paragraph.

Test 1

Section 7: Math

Question: 1
Answer: E

Count the number of houses depicted for:
1961 - 1970 (2)
1971 - 1980 (4)
1981 - 1990 (8)
They total 14 houses, and each house represents 2,000 new homes. Multiply 14 by 2,000 and you get your answer: 28,000

Question: 2
Answer: B

Remember that vertical (opposite) angles are equal. So opposite the 35 degree angle, moving into the triangle, is another 35 degree angle. Opposite the 45 degree angle, moving into the triangle, is another 45 degree angle. Since the three angles of any triangle must total 180 degrees, simply put 180 in your calculator, deduct 35 and deduct 45. You are left with the measure of angle w, which is 100 degrees.

Question: 3
Answer: E

There are 19 tables in the restaurant. At least four people are going to sit at each table. So multiply 19 times 4 to get 76.....the number of people who are seated when four people are at each table.

Since the restaurant can hold 84 people, deduct 76 from 84 to get 8....the number of people who still need to be seated. Have each of these 8 people join a table of 4, and you will have 8 tables seating 5 people.

Question: 4
Answer: D

Substitute 4 in for a, and you will have: 4m squared + 4m + 4
Factor out the 4 and you will have: 4(m squared +m +1)

Question: 5
Answer: A

Since the circle touches all sides of the square, the diameter of the circle is equal to the side of the square, which is 2. The radius is always half of the diameter, so the radius of the circle is 1. (Whenever they ask the area of a circle, they have to give you a way to find the radius so you can use the formula for the area of a circle, which is pie times the radius squared)
The area of the circle is therefore pie times 1 squared, which is simply pie.
Since one quarter of the circle is shaded, the area of the shaded portion is ¼ times pie, or pie divided by 4.

Question: 6
Answer: C

The rule you need to remember is that slopes of perpendicular lines are negative reciprocals. The equation given is: x + 3y = 12. Subtract x from both sides to get: 3y = -x +12. Divide both sides by 3 to get: y = -1/3x + 4.
Since the slope is the number before x, it is clear that the slope of the given line is - 1/3. The slope of a perpendicular line must be the negative reciprocal, or +3. The only choice, among the answers offered, with a slope of +3 is C, so that must be the answer.

Question: 7
Answer: E

There is a geometric rule that the sum of any two sides of a triangle must be greater than the third side. If two sides of a triangle are each 5, their sum is 10, which must be greater than the length of the third side. The third side must therefore be less than 10.

Question: 8
Answer: C

Write an equation. Candidate II got x votes. Candidate I got x + 28,000 votes. Total votes cast was 2.8 million. So equation is:
x + x + 28,000 = 2,800,000
2x + 28,000 = 2,800,000
2x = 2,772,000
x = 1,386,000
Since Candidate I got x + 28,000 votes, Candidate I got 1,414,000 votes
We are asked what percent of the 2.8 million votes Candidate I got.
So the answer is 1,414,000 divided by 2,800,000 which is .505
That is the same as 50.5 percent.

Question: 9
Answer: 9

Square both sides of the equation.
You now have: 2p = 18
Divide both sides by 2 and find P = 9

Question: 10
Answer: .2 or 1/5

1.783 rounded to the nearest whole number is 2
1.783 rounded to the nearest tenth is 1.8

We are being asked the difference.
2 – 1.8 = .2

Question: 11
Answer: 15

If the probability of choosing a brown towel is 2/5, then 2/5 of the towels are brown. We are told there are six brown towels. So the equation is:
2/5 x = 6 Divide both sides by 2/5 to get x = 15 (the number of towels in the closet)

Question: 12
Answer: any positive number less than 1.5 (or less than 3/2)

We are told the length of line segment BE is 3.5
Line segment BE can be broken down into 3 parts, BC, CD and DE.
We are told that CD is equal to 2.
So the sum of BC and DE is equal to 1.5
The length of BC can therefore be any number small than 1.5 (or smaller than 3/2 if you write your answer as a fraction).

Question: 13
Answer: 6

We are told that it rained for 3 out of every 5 days in April (3/5 of days)
We are told it did not rain for 2 out of every 5 days in April (2/5 of days)
Since there are 30 days in April, solve that 3/5 of 30 equals 18. Solve that 2/5 of 30 equals 12. The difference between 18 and 12 is 6.

Question: 14
Answer: 117

There are three "terms" between the third and the sixth terms. Since the third term is 17 and the sixth term is 77, get the difference between the two numbers (77-17 is 60). So the difference between the 3 terms is 60. Divide 60 by 3 to get 20, the difference between any two terms. So if the sixth term is 77, add 20 to get the seventh term, which would be 97. Then add 20 to get the eighth term (and answer!) which is 117.

Question: 15
Answer: 2.5 or 5/2

Absolute value means the difference from zero.
So x-3 can either equal positive ½ or x-3 can equal negative ½.
Solve for both.
If x-3 = ½, then x = 3.5   If x-3 = -1/2, then x = 2.5
They are asking for the least value, so the answer is 2.5 (or 5/2)

Question: 16
Answer: 5940

This is a reasoning question. Since X is the sum of the other 3 digits, it has to be the largest digit. So try 9 (the largest one digit number).
W is one more than Y (Don't forget that all 3 digits have to total 9)
When you try making W equal to 5, which would make Y equal to 4, it all works out. Z is W-5 (5-5) or zero.
So WXYZ is equal to 5940.

Question: 17
Answer: 90

Remember that all three triangles are equilateral.

Line segments CD, DE and EF are all 10 inches in length. That makes CE (the side of one triangle) equal to 20 inches, so BC is also 20 inches, and ½ of BE (the solid line) would be 10 inches.
Do the same with the other large triangle.
Since DF is 20 inches, AF is also 20 inches, and ½ of AD (the solid line) would be 10 inches.
Add up all of the solid lines and they total 90 inches.

Question: 18
Answer: 4.2 or 21/5

Look at the graph and note that at the point where x = 3, y = 0
They tell us that g(a - 1.2) = 0
Therefore, a - 1.2 = 3
Add 1.2 to both sides and find that a = 4.2

Test 1

Section 8: Math

Question: 1
Answer: D

The honorable mention ribbons are depicted by the shaded bars of the graph. There are 4 for painting, 2 for pottery, 5 for photography, 1 for metalwork and 1 for silkscreen. Adding these numbers together will give you an answer of 13.

Question: 2
Answer: E

Since the radii of the circle are all equal, line segments AB, AC, AD and AE are all equal (congruent). Since two sides of triangle ABC are congruent to two sides of triangle ADE, the third sides must also be congruent. Line segment BC, which is 4, is equal to line segment DE, which therefore must also be 4.

Question: 3
Answer: A

This is a substitution problem. Substitute 5 or a, 2 for b, and 6 for c.
You now need to find the value of 5 squared – (5 times 6) + 6. Simplify to 25 – 30 + 6 which equals 1.

Question: 4
Answer: C

Draw the x and y axis, then plot the given points, as well as the points of the other two vertices, which are (2, -2) and (-2, 2). Connect the dots and you will have a square with sides of length 4. The area of a square is length times width, so 4 x 4 = 16.

Question: 5
Answer: B

All of the necessary information is given, just in a mixed up order. We are told that Steph is the youngest child. We are told that Owen has an older brother and sister, so he is therefore the second youngest child. We are told that Chadd is not the oldest, so he comes next, leaving Daria to be the oldest child.

Question: 6
Answer: E

In a parallelogram, the angles in the positions marked by x and y always add up to 180 degrees. We are asked the value of 2 times (x + y).
Two times 180 equals 360.

Question: 7
Answer: A

If 3 numbers average 12, they add up to 3 times 12, or 36.
Therefore the first equation is: $x + y + z = 36$.
Next, they want us to subtract the largest number (z) from the sum of the other two numbers (x + y) and get 4.
Therefore, the second equation is: $x + y - z = 4$.
These equations are paired together in choice A.

Question: 8
Answer: B

First, look at the left side of the equation. When you multiply numbers with exponents, if the base number is the same, you add the exponents. So (3 to the 2x power) times (3 to the 2y power) equals 3 to the 2x +2y power.
Next, look at the right side of the equation. Change 81 to 3 to the fourth power.
Now set them equal. Since both sides have 3 as the base number, the exponents must be equal. So $2x + 2y = 4$
Factor out the 2 and get $2(x + y) = 4$
Divide both sides by 2 and get $x + y = 2$

Question: 9
Answer: B

When you look at the graph you see that the graph reaches its highest value when the x value is 4, halfway between 2 and 6, where it crosses the x axis at both points.

Question: 10
Answer: B

Cross multiply to find that x = 3K
Multiply both sides by 3 to find that 3x = 9K

Question: 11
Answer: A

There are 6 "faces" on a cube. If 2 are black, and the rest are white, there are 4 white faces.
If the total area of the white faces is 64 square inches, divide 64 by 4 to find the area of each face.
Since each face has an area of 16 square inches, each side is 4 inches. (Remember the area of a square is side times side.)
Since all the sides are 4, the volume is 4 x 4 x 4 = 64.

Question: 12
Answer: B

Using the markings on the number line, give each variable a value.
Note that: v = -.75   w = -.5   x = .25   y = .75
Using your calculator to find the value of each answer choice, you will find that B is the least value at -.5

Question: 13
Answer: D

Do not overlook the sentence that says that n is an integer (whole number). Remember that "median" means middle.
If you add an integer equal or less than 6, then 6 would be the median of the new list of 7 numbers.
If you add an integer equal or greater than 7, then 7 would be the median of the new list of 7 numbers.
The new number added to the list cannot be 6 ½ because that is not an integer. And 6 ½ is not currently listed.
So the median of the new list could be either 6 or 7.

Question: 14
Answer: B

You have 5 available color choices. So you can choose any of 5 colors to paint the two sections labeled "Color 1." Once you use 1 of the colors, you then have a choice of the 4 remaining colors to paint the middle section labeled "Color 2." To find the number of possible color combinations, you multiply 5 (the possibilities for color 1) by 4 (the possibilities for color 2) to get an answer of 20.

Question: 15
Answer: E

Draw a rectangle and assign a width and length that is easy to calculate. e.g. length = 10 and width = 20
The area would be 200.
(Remember area of a rectangle is equal to length x width.)
Now follow their directions and increase the length by 30%
The new length would be 13.
Follow their directions and decrease the width by 30%
The new width would be 14.
Calculate the new area. 13 x 14 = 182
Since the area changed from 200 to 182, it decreased.
It decreased by 18/200 which is 9%.

Question: 16
Answer: B

When you substitute 10 for t, you get the equation:
$n(10) = 50 - 200 + k$ or $n(10) = -150 + k$
When you substitute in the other answer choices, the only one that comes out with the same answer is 30.
Note that: $n(30) = 450 - 600 + k$ or $n(30) = -150 + k$

Test 1

Section 9: Critical Reading

Question: 1
Answer: B

Vocabulary:
A) imprecise (inaccurate, vague, ill-defined)
B) **straightforward (direct, forthright, up-front)**
C) deficient (lacking, scarce)
D) obtrusive (obvious, conspicuous)
E) elliptical (egg-shaped, oval)

If it is "free of tricks or evasiveness" (indirectness), then it is direct or straightforward.

Question: 2
Answer: C

Vocabulary:
A) vast (massive, enormous), hollow (empty)
B) sparse (scarce), thunderous (deafening, very loud)
C) **enormous (massive, huge), deafening (very loud)**
D) unimpressive (not impressive or inspiring, average), muted (subdued, low-key, quiet)
E) negligible (unimportant, insignificant) rousing (stimulating, inspiring)

If the team was very popular, then the size of the crowd must be very large, which would limit the first blank choice to vast (A) or enormous (C). The cheers would likely be very loud, which would, for the second blank, eliminate (A) and make the best choice (C).

Question: 3
Answer: B

Vocabulary:
A) advanced (sophisticated, superior), setback (holdup, stumbling block)
B) **altered (changed), revolution (rebellion, transformation)**

61

C) contradicted (opposed, disproved), truce (cease-fire, peaceful break)
D) reinforced (strengthened, secured), crisis (catastrophe, emergency)
E) halted (stopped), breakthrough (advance, discovery)

Substitute in the word choices, and eliminate any that do not fit, either due to the first or the second blank. The only pair of words that would logically fit and those in choice (B). The first blank could be filled in with a word that means "changed," while the second blank could be filled in with a word that means "transformation."

Question: 4
Answer: E

Vocabulary:
A) credence (belief, credibility), irrefutable (indisputable, convincing)
B) disrepute (disgrace), dubious (doubtful, uncertain)
C) acceptance (receiving, approval), convincing (credible, believable)
D) momentum (energy, drive), systematic (methodical, organized)
E) currency (prevalence or money), inconclusive (uncertain)

The sentence begins with the word "although," so we know there has to be a contrast within the sentence. If we substitute in the pairs of words, the only pair that works is (E). The sentence then states that the theory has gain "currency," meaning it is prevalent or widely believed, but the evidence is still "inconclusive" or uncertain.

Question: 5
Answer: B

Vocabulary:
A) palpable (tangible, real)
B) diaphanous (transparent, sheer)
C) variegated (multi-colored)
D) luxurious (lavish, expensive)
E) anomalous (unusual, uncharacteristic, atypical)

This is a straight forward vocabulary questions. What word means transparent? Eliminate any words that you know do not fit, and then, if necessary, take a good guess.

Question: 6
Answer: D

Vocabulary:
A) an egalitarian (a person who believes in equality)
B) a dowager (a wealthy widow)
C) a dilettante (a person who pretends to appreciate the arts)
D) an iconoclast (a person one who challenges tradition)
E) a purveyor (a vendor or provider of goods)

This again, is a straight forward vocabulary question. If you don't know the answer, but can narrow down the choices, take a good guess.

Question: 7
Answer: C

This entire story is about a confrontation between two people who, as it states in the first paragraph, "had characters that would not harmonize." Since they had an opposite view on everything, we can say that their "differences seemed irreconcilable."

Question: 8
Answer: C

We are told in the first paragraph that she was "spirited,"…..
"liked freedom"….and was "romantic." Since none of the other
answer choices were referred to, (C) is the only possible
answer.

Question: 9
Answer: E

It states in the introductory paragraph that Mr. Sympson was
her guardian until she reached adulthood. Then, in the
referenced lines (8-11), it states that he wants to get his niece
married to a "proper husband" and "wash his hands of her
forever." Clearly, he no longer wants to be responsible for her.

Question: 10
Answer: E

The referenced lines described the potential husband as
having an "unencumbered estate" and "good connections,"
which are references to financial and social advantages.

Question: 11
Answer: A

In the referenced lines, it says that Mr. Wynne has "run a
course of despicable, commonplace profligacy." Eliminate the
choices that are just off-topic, which would get rid of most of
them. Even if you don't know the meaning of the unusual
work "profligacy," which means wastefulness or extravagance,
you could probably match up "undignified" in Choice A with
"commonplace" in the referenced line, giving you a good idea
of the correct answer.

Question: 12
Answer: B

In the referenced lines, Miss Keeldar is asked whether she ever plans to marry. Her answer is, "I deny your right to claim an answer to that question." Basically, she is saying, "I don't have to tell you. It's none of your business." That matches up with Choice B.

Question: 13
Answer: D

In the referenced lines, Mr. Sympson warns Miss Keeldar to "be on your guard!....I will not be trifled with!" But in the introductory information, prior to the start of the story, we are told that Mr. Sympson WAS her guardian until she reached adulthood. Therefore he no longer has any authority over her.

Question: 14
Answer: A

Prior to the referenced lines, Mr. Sympson warned Miss Keeldar, with trembling hand and voice, to "take care." She responds in the referenced lines, that she will take "scrupulous care" NOT to marry someone who she does not admire and love. She is turning around the meaning of Mr. Sympson's warning.

Question: 15
Answer: D

After Miss Keeldar states that she knows she is speaking in an "unknown tongue," she says that she is indifferent (doesn't care) whether or not Mr. Sympson comprehends (understands) her.

Question: 16
Answer: B

When Mr. Sympson poses the question, "To what will she come?" we are told that he "lifted his hands and eyes toward heaven." The implication is that things look so bad that she needs God's help!

Question: 17
Answer: C

Miss Keeldar responds the rhetorical question as if it were a real question, and replies that a wedding to Sam Wynne is not in her future.

Question: 18
Answer: B

In several parts of the story, Miss Keeldar makes it very clear that she intends to marry for love. In fact, in line 84 she states that she plans "to love with my whole heart." Therefore, it is obvious that she views love as a "crucial prerequisite" (necessary condition) to an acceptable marriage.

Question: 19
Answer: E

Throughout the passage we get the sense that the Mr. Sympson is most concerned that a potential husband has plenty of money, and Miss Keeldar is most concerned that he is cultured. Therefore, they both agree that she should not marry a man who lacks money and culture, or, in other words, "is poor and undignified."

Test 1

Section 10: Writing

Question: 1
Answer: D

Since the word "challenges" is plural, the verb before it must be "are" not "is." That narrows the choices down to D and E, with D being grammatically correct.

Question: 2
Answer: C

The sentence is in the present tense with C being the simplest, most straightforward wording.

Question: 3
Answer: B

Since three presidents are named, we have to say "presidencies." This narrows the choices to B and D, with B being grammatically correct.

Question: 4
Answer: E

This sentence is ambiguous. Since two females are named, we cannot say "she noticed." We must name one specifically. As for the verb, "noticed" is parallel with "visited."

Question: 5
Answer: C

This sentence starts out by saying, "carried by the strong, dry winds of the stratosphere..." The next word must state exactly what was carried, and it was "dust," which narrows the choices to C and D. C is the correct choice, because we don't want the word "that" prior to the word "crossed."

Question: 6
Answer: E

The two parts of the sentence can only be linked by the word "that," making E the correct choice.

Question: 7
Answer: D

The shift….is occurring because…...   Choice D is the only grammatically correct way of wording this present tense sentence.

Question: 8
Answer: E

The sentence starts by saying, "If asked to name a musical group….." Who is being asked? People are being asked. So the underlined portion must start with "many people….."

Question: 9
Answer: E

We are talking about the year 1972, so the sentence is in the past tense. Choice E is the simplest, most direct way of wording the sentence.

Question: 10
Answer: A

This sentence is correct the way it is, in the most straightforward, grammatically correct form.

Question: 11
Answer: D

The sentence starts with, "The newspaper business…..faces a challenge"……… The next word must be "because," making D the correct answer.

Question: 12
Answer: D

We are looking for parallel sentence structure here. "Adults are overharvested......eggs are disturbed.....nesting habitats are destroyed."

Question: 13
Answer: C

The sentence names two factors (plural) that "contribute," making C the correct answer.

Question: 14
Answer: E

This sentence requires parallel sentence structure. Alexei is annoying "because of his unpredictability" AND delightful "because of his imagination."

Test 2

Section 2: Math

Question: 1
Answer: D

To go from one number to the next in the sequence you need to double the number an add 2. Therefore:
   1 times 2 = 2 Add 2 and get 4
   4 times 2 = 8 Add 2 and get 10
 10 times 2 = 20 Add 2 and get 22

Question: 2
Answer: A

Since they want the answer in minutes, convert the 1 hour to 60 minutes. Now we have a ratio (or proportion) question.
24 cartons in 60 minutes = x cartons in 5 minutes
24/60 = x/5
Cross multiply: 24 times 5 = 60x

120 = 60x
Divide both sides by 60 to find 2 = x

Question: 3
Answer: A

Look at the graph.
In the month of May, 48 cars were sold.
In the months of January and February combined, 20 + 18, or 38, cars were sold.
The difference between 48 and 38 (48 – 38) is 10.

Question: 4
Answer: C

Look at the graph.
In the month of April, 30 cars were sold.
In all six months combined, 180 cars were sold.
(20 + 18 + 22 + 30 + 48 + 42 = 180)
Since there are 360 degrees in a circle, if this were illustrated by a circle graph the ratio would be:
30/180 = x/360
Cross multiply
30 times 360 = 180x
10,800 = 180X
Divide both sides by 180
X = 60

Question: 5
Answer: D

Look at the figure and picture what it would look like if the side now facing the top of the page was rotated (turned) to be facing the left side of the page. What would the new figure look like? Figure D.

Question: 6
Answer: D

Write out the equation.
Three more than twice a number can be written as: 2x + 3
So the equation is: 2x + 3 = 10
Subtract 3 from both sides to find 2x = 7.
The question asks, "what is 4 times the number"
In other words, what is 4x
Since we know that 2x = 7, we multiply both sides of the
equation by 2 to find 4x = 14

Question: 7
Answer: A

Since a < 0, give a any negative value and plug it in to the
choices. The greatest (largest) number is going to be a.
When you multiply a negative number by a positive number,
you get a negative number. The larger the positive number,
the smaller the product.

Question: 8
Answer: B

To get the area of an irregular figure, separate it into two
regular figures. Look at the line segment that measures "2"
and extend it across the figure.
You now have a rectangle on top that measures 2 by 6, and a
square below it that measures 4 by 4.
You calculate area by multiplying length by width.
The area of the rectangle is 2 times 6 = 12
The area of the square is 4 times 4 = 16
Add the two separate areas to get the area of the total figure.
12 + 16 = 28

Question: 9
Answer: D

Get the square root of both sides and you will have:
X – 2 = positive or negative 5   Solve for both:

When X − 2 = positive 5,   X = 7
When X − 2 = negative 5,   X = -3
They state that X is less than zero, so X = -3

Question: 10
Answer: E

The two triangles are similar, so the sides are in proportion.
The ratio of side QT to side RS is equal to the ratio of side PT to side PS.
We are given the value of side QT as 8 and side RS as 10.
So the ratio is 8/10 which can be reduced to 4/5.
That is therefore the same ratio for PT/PS.

Question: 11
Answer: D

Pick a few points on the graph to get the relationship between the length and the week.
Note: the length is 10 at week 1,
          the length is 30 at week 3,
          the length is 50 at week 5
This pattern shows that the length = 10 times the week.
So L = 10W

Question: 12
Answer: A

Put the numbers in order and you have: 5, 5, 5, 5, 6, 6, 6, 7 and n.
Remember that mode means the number repeated the most times.
Median means the number in the middle.
They state that the only mode is 5, and there are four 5's, so n cannot equal 6 because there are currently three sixes and if you add another one you would have four 6's and that would be another mode.

Any number greater than 6 would work because 5 would still be the only mode and 6 would be the median.

Question: 13
Answer: C

Look at the Venn diagram and notice where circles Y and Z overlap. There are two segments that are in both circles. One has 3 elements and one has 7 elements. Add them together to get an answer of 10.

Question: 14
Answer: E

Substitute t^3 in for m.
You then solve that $w = t^3$ squared plus t^3
Since t^3 squared is equal to t^6, the answer is t^6 plus t^3

Question: 15
Answer: B

First of all, substitute 6 for x and find that $(6-1)(6+1) = 35$
Then substitute 5 for x and find that $(5-1)(5+1) = 24$
So $35 - 24 = 11$ which is the answer.
But which of the potential answers is the same as 11?
When you plug in the possible answers you find that B is the one that works.
Substitute 3 for x and find that $(3-1)(3+1) = 8$
Substitute 2 for x and find that $(2-1)(2+1) = 3$
Since $8 + 3 = 11$ you have your answer.

Question: 16
Answer: D

Try the answers and see which one works. First of all, it says that x/y is NOT an integer. When you try the answers, that is true for B (3/2 is NOT an integer) and D (6/4 is NOT an integer).

Next, it says that x^2/y IS an integer. When you try choice B you get 3^2/2 which equals 9/2 and is NOT an integer so it cannot be the correct answer.
Then confirm that D works. 6^2/4 equals 36/4 which is 9 and IS an integer so it is the correct answer.

Question: 17
Answer: B

Look at the graph and note that the absolute value of any graph takes the parts of the graph that are negative (below the x axis) and reflects them across the x-axis. Since absolute values are always positive, every point on the graph has to have a positive Y value. This eliminates choices A, C and E. Choice B reflects the line from the point where it hits the X axis, and is therefore the correct answer.

Question: 18
Answer: B

The smallest rectangular box that totally contains the cylinder would have a length and width of d and a height of h. The formula for the volume of a rectangular solid is length x width x height, which in this case is d x d x h or d^2 h.

Question: 19
Answer: E

Write out two equations from the information provided.
$X^2 = 4(y^2)$ and $X = 2y+1$
Next, square both sides of the second equation to get: $X^2 = (2y+1)^2$
Since $X^2 = 4(y^2)$ and $X^2 = (2y+1)^2$ then $4(y^2) = (2y+1)^2$
Next, foil the right side of the equation to get:
$4(y^2) = 4(y^2) + 4y + 1$
Subtract $4(y^2)$ from both sides.
Now we have: $0 = 4y+1$
Subtract 1 from both sides to get: $-1 = 4y$

Divide both sides by 4 to get: Y= -1/4
Since the question asks the value of X, we need to plug the value of Y into one of the equations. Let's use the equation X = 2y + 1.
X = 2(-1/4) + 1   which totals ½.

Question: 20
Answer: E

The slopes of perpendicular lines are negative reciprocals. First, get the slope of line l, which is the difference in the y coordinates divided by the difference in the x coordinates.
So the slope of line l is 1-0/2-0 which is ½
Therefore the slope of line q must be -2 (which is the negative reciprocal)
Since line q contains points (2, 1) and (0, t) we can solve for t with the equation that -2 (the slope) = 1-t/2-0
So -2 = 1-t/2
Cross multiply to get -4 = 1-t
Subtract 1 from both sides to get -5 = -t
So 5 = t.

Test 2

Section 4: Critical Reading

Question: 1
Answer: C

> Vocabulary:
> A) convincing (persuasive), misinterpret (misunderstand)
> B) misleading (deceiving, confusing), anticipate (foresee, predict)
> **C) predictable (expected), foresee (anticipate, predict)**
> D) ironic (satirical, mocking), endorse (validate, support)

E) spellbinding (captivating, riveting), ignore (disregard)

It's easiest to solve for the second blank first. If you knew what was going to happen, you could anticipate or foresee villain's fate. This narrows the possibilities down to B or C. The first blank could therefore be predictable, but not misleading.

Question: 2
Answer: B

Vocabulary:
A) liquefying (becoming a liquid), founder (sink, submerge)
B) **contaminating (polluting), backfire (fail, disappoint)**
C) purifying (making clean), boomerang (rebound, ricochet)
D) saturating (wetting thoroughly), reciprocate (repay, give back)
E) polluting (contaminating), prevail ((win, triumph)

In the context of the sentence, the first blank has to mean contaminating or polluting, narrowing down the possible answers to B or E. For the second blank, the correct answer has to be backfire or boomerang, which are choices B and C. So the only answer that works for both blanks is choice B.

Question: 3
Answer: A

Vocabulary:
A) dispassionate (without emotion)
B) insubstantial (weak)
C) esoteric (abstract)
D) capricious (unpredictable)
E) Indignant (angry, furious)

The end of the sentence says it was lacking any emotion, which is the definition of dispassionate. If you analyze the word, "dis" means "not" and "passion" means "great emotion or feeling."

Question: 4
Answer: B

Vocabulary:
A) Conclusive (decisive, convincing), reality (the way things actually are)
B) **Tenable (can be supported, defended or justified), misconception (false idea)**
C) Mythical (imaginary, legendary), possibility (likelihood)
D) Erroneous (wrong, incorrect), delusion (false impression)
E) Hypothetical (supposed, presumed), digression (straying, deviation)

The second part of the sentence says that the belief that the Taino people died out must be _____ since there are modern descendants. So the word for this blank must be either misconception or delusion, making the possible answers B or D. The first blank can certainly be tenable, but cannot be erroneous, so B is the correct answer.

Question: 5
Answer: E

Vocabulary:
A) Substantiated (supported, upheld)
B) Impugned (challenged, called into question)
C) Protected (safeguarded)
D) United (combined)
E) **Mollified (calmed down, soothed)**

This is a matter of knowing the vocabulary. The context of the sentence calls for a word that means "calmed down" or "soothed," which is the meaning of mollified.

Question: 6
Answer: A

Vocabulary:
A) Flotsam (wreckage, floating remains)
B) Reconnaissance (investigation, exploration)
C) Decimation (destruction, killing)
D) Raiment (clothing, apparel)
E) Sustenance (nourishment)

Basically, we want a word that means "garbage" to fill in the blank. If you don't know the word "flotsam," which is an unusual word, try to eliminate the words that you know don't work and back into the correct answer.

Question: 7
Answer: A

Vocabulary:
A) Disposition (temperament, character), cantankerous (irritable, short-tempered)
B) Anatomy (physical makeup), churlish (ill-mannered, rude)
C) Outlook (viewpoint, perspective), benevolent (kind-hearted)
D) Personality (character, temperament), laconic (concise, using very few words)
E) Stature (importance, prominence, height), robust (healthy, energetic, vigorous)

The sentence starts by saying that aging brings about physical changes, but does not change a person's _____. So the words that would work for the first blank are "disposition" and "personality," limiting the possible answers to A and D. The second part of the sentence calls for a synonym for "irascible," which means "easily angered." Cantankerous works, making the correct answer A. "Laconic," which means "using very few words," eliminates choice D.

Question: 8
Answer: A

> Vocabulary:
> **A) Mercurial (temperamental, changeable, unpredictable)**
> B) Corrosive (eroding)
> C) Disingenuous (insincere, deceitful)
> D) Implacable (cannot be calmed down or appeased)
> E) Phlegmatic (calm, composed)

The context of the sentence makes it clear that we need a word that means unpredictable, changeable or temperamental. That is the definition of mercurial!

Question: 9
Answer: D

The difference between the two passages is the view of the relationship between "empty" land and the overcrowding of the planet. The answer to this question is therefore "D" because the author of Passage 2 believes that the author of Passage 1 incorrectly focusses on population density in considering whether the Earth is overcrowded.

Question: 10
Answer: C

The first sentence of Passage 2 ends with the words "it is wrong." That can certainly be considered "emphatic" as it unmistakably states a definite point of view.

Question: 11
Answer: C

The author puts the word "empty" in quotes and then spends the rest of the sentence stating what the land is used for – emphasizing the fact that the land is not, actually, "empty."

Question: 12
Answer: A

Both authors agree that there is a plenty of unoccupied land on Earth. The author of Passage 1 states this in the second sentence. The author of Passage 2 discusses this throughout the last half of the passage.

Question: 13
Answer: B

Strategy: After reading the introduction, read the passage, one paragraph at a time, answering the questions as you go. The map that is being unrolled is described as if it is alive, so the correct answer is "animate," which means "living, alive, breathing."

Question: 14
Answer: C

The narrator is describing the impression that he is getting from Lewis' hand as it moves over the map. He states, for example, that when Lewis' hand stops moving, it seems as though the streams stop running.

Question: 15
Answer: D

The narrator describes Lewis' hand as having "power over the terrain." His hand is described as having the power to make "streams everywhere quit running." The hands are described as all-powerful or invincible, which is the definition of "omnipotent."

Question: 16
Answer: E

The narrator says that the "streams everywhere quit running, hanging silently." That's saying that the streams are NOT moving, but are "suspended" as they wait for Lewis to stop talking!

Question: 17
Answer: E

The valley is described as being "wild" when it is compared to Alaska. Wild land is "undeveloped."

Question: 18
Answer: A

Lewis wants to get to see the land before the real estate people ruin it (by developing the land). He is therefore "contemptuous" (scornful, disdainful) towards the real estate people.

Question: 19
Answer: E

Lewis wants the land to remain wild. So he is being sarcastic, or "ironic" when he says that the real estate people are going to develop it into "heaven".... a place of eternal happiness.

Question: 20
Answer: B

In lines 25 to 30, the narrator looks at the map "trying to see the changes that would come"…………."and also trying to visualize the land as Lewis said it was at the moment." The narrator is therefore picturing two very different conditions.

Question: 21
Answer: A

The narrator says that his body, "particularly the back and arms, felt ready for something like this." He is physically ready for this canoe trip.

Question: 22
Answer: A

The narrator looks at the map, "picking up the river where we would enter it." The narrator is clearly "locating" the spot where they would start their canoe trip.

Question: 23
Answer: D

The narrator implies that he is about to get a lesson or a lecture from Lewis, who in the previous sentence had given the narrator a look to imply that he was being tolerant of him. Lewis is being portrayed as being "didactic," which means "informative, instructional, educational."

Question: 24
Answer: C

In lines 48 to 51 it says that Lewis likes to "take some extremely specialized and difficult form of sport…and evolve a personal approach."

Question: 25
Answer: C

In the sentence prior to this paragraph, it states that Bobby doesn't take Lewis very seriously. In lines 63 to 66, Bobby says that when the average person gets an urge to do something like this (canoe trip), he usually lies down until he changes his mind. This is an example of dry humor, which is humor that is witty or sarcastic. Lewis responds with more dry humor, saying people are usually dead (Woodlawn, we are told, is a cemetery) "before they think of getting up."

Test 2

Section 5: Math

Question: 1
Answer: B

First, solve for X
If $3x = 0$, divide both sides by 3 to find that $x = 0$.
Substitute 0 in for x and find that $1 + 0 = 0 = 1$

Question: 2
Answer: E

The diameter of a circle is directly related to the radius since the diameter is always twice the radius.
So if the ratio of the diameter of circle A to the diameter of circle B is 3 to 1, then the ratio of the radius of circle A to the radius of circle B is likewise 3 to 1, which is written 3 : 1.

Question: 3
Answer: D

Picture a set of numbers whose average is 3.
The numbers could all be 3
The numbers could be 2, 3 and 4.
The numbers could be 1, 2, 3, 4 and 5, or countless other varieties.

But if you double all of the numbers in a set that average 3, your new average will be 6.

Question: 4
Answer: C

When you multiply a number by 10^{-2} it is the same as dividing the number by 10^2
10^2 is equal to 100
PRT divided by 100 is equal to P.RT

Question: 5
Answer: E

Substitute any number at all for k.
If you add "n" (any other number) to k and end up with a smaller number, then you must have added a negative number.
Therefore n < 0.

Question: 6
Answer: A

We are given the slope as 7/16.
Slope is the difference between the y coordinates of two points divided by the difference between the x coordinates of two points.
At the bottom of the ramp the coordinates are (0, 0)
At the top of the ramp the coordinates are (x, 3.5)
So the slope, 7/16, is equal to 3.5/x
Cross multiply to get 7x = 56
Divide both sides by 7 to find that x = 8.

Question: 7
Answer: B

We are given the graph of the pictured parabola as $y = ax^2 + 2$
The "2" represents the y intercept.

The "a" determines the shape of the parabola. Larger values make the parabola narrower, while smaller values make the parabola wider.

In the second equation of $y = (a/3)(x^2) + 2$ we have the same y intercept, but the value of "a" becomes "a/3" so the shape of the new parabola will be wider.

Question: 8
Answer: B

This is a probability question.

If Meredith chooses the color of her hat first, she has 3 choices (red, white or blue).

Next, if she chooses the color of sweater, she has two choices left.

Lastly, for the color of her jeans, she will have only one choice.

As with all probability questions, take the number of possibilities for each one separately, and multiply them.

Therefore, $3 \times 2 \times 1 = 6$.

Question: 9
Answer: 4.5 OR 9/2

Turns the words into an equation and you will have:
$2x + 5 = 14$
Subtract 5 from both sides and you will have:
$2x = 9$
Divide both sides by 2 and you will have:
$x = 9/2$ or 4.5

Question: 10
Answer: 135

Since lines l and m are parallel, the angles on the same side of the transversal, marked "x" and "y," are called "same side interior angles" and they add up to 180 degrees.

So $x + y = 180$.

We are told that y = 3x, so substitute 3x for y and the new equation will be:
x + 3x = 180 or 4x = 180
Divide both sides by 4 and get x = 45
Since they are asking the value of y (or 3x)
y = 3(45) or 135.

Question: 11
Answer: 32

This problem deals with volume.
To find the number of CD cases that will fit in the box, find the volume of each. Then divide the volume of the box by the volume of a CD case.
Volume of the box is: 4 x 4 x 8 = 128
Volume of a CD case is: 4 x 4 x ¼ = 4
128/4 = 32

Question: 12
Answer: 1/15, .066, or .067

Look at the equation and set 6 = 3x + y, and 5 = y
Substitute 5 in for y and get 6 = 3x + 5
Subtract 5 from both sides and get:
1 = 3x
Divide both sides by 3 and get:
X = 1/3
The question asks the value of x/y.
Substitute 1/3 for x and 5 for y and get 1/3 divided by 5 or 1/15
Correct answers in decimal form are: .066 or .067

Question: 13
Answer: 1750

To find the average increase in profits over 3 years, first find the total increase in profits (26,250 – 21,000) and then divide by 3.
5,250/3 = 1,750

Question: 14
Answer: 4.25<X<8.5 OR 17/4<X<17/2

This question is asking what number you can find that, when plugged into the equation, will leave you with a smaller number. The integers what will work are 5, 6 and 7.
Consider 5, for example
$f(5) = [3(5) - 17]$
$f(5) = [15 - 17] = 2$
Since 2 is less than 5, it is one of the correct answers.
Any number greater than 4.25 and less than 8.5 is correct.

Question: 15
Answer: 8

RED	GREEN
25	25
-3	-4
22	21

The chart above shows where Ari is after taking 3 red and 4 green pieces from the candy jar. He now takes an additional 13 pieces. By taking 7 red and 6 green pieces, he will have an equal number of pieces of each color. But by taking 8 red pieces, he will have more red than green pieces. So the answer is 8.

Question: 16
Answer: 9

We must find the number of 3 consecutive integers which, when multiplied, will equal a number less than 1,000. Let's list the possibilities:
$1 \times 2 \times 3 = 6$
$2 \times 3 \times 4 = 24$

3 x 4 x 5 = 60
4 x 5 x 6 = 120
5 x 6 x 7 = 210
6 x 7 x 8 = 336
7 x 8 x 9 = 504
8 x 9 x 10 = 720
9 x 10 x 11 = 990
There are 9 possible answers.

Question: 17
Answer: 40

Let's write an equation to solve this:
$1 + .07(t-20) = .06t$
Distribute to get:
$1 + .07t - 1.4 = .06t$
Combine like terms:
$-.4 + .07t = .06t$
Subtract .07t from both sides:
$-.4 = -.01t$
Divide both sides by -.01
$40 = t$

Question: 18
Answer: 8/5 OR 1.6

It states that the perimeter equals the area. So find the perimeter and find the area, and then set them equal to each other.
Since the length of each side is k, the perimeter is equal to 16k
Since the length of each side is k, the area of each square is k^2
There are 10 squares, so the total area is $10k^2$.
Set the perimeter equal to the area and get:
$16K = 10k^2$
Divide both sides by 10k

Find k = 1.6 or 8/5 (Remember you always have to reduce your answer!)

Test 2

Section 6: Writing

Question: 1
Answer: D

Since we need parallel sentence structure, the words "reading and relaxing" are parallel with "practicing. That narrows down the answer to choices to A, B and D, with only D being grammatically correct.

Question: 2
Answer: E

Read the sentence, eliminating the clause "winner….Medicine," and you will have "Sir Ronald Ross identified…." making the correct choice E.

Question: 3
Answer: C

The sentence starts out by saying "Traveling through Yosemite," so the next word has to state exactly who was traveling through Yosemite. That word would be "we," narrowing down the choices to C and D, with C being grammatically correct.

Question: 4
Answer: C

The directions to this section state that they want the sentences to be "clear and precise." Substituting the underlined words with the words "to recount" is the simplest way to achieve this.

Question: 5
Answer: B

Choice B is simple, direct and grammatically correct.

Question: 6
Answer: C

In order to have parallel sentence structure, we have to choose a sentence with the word "influenced" which is parallel with "shaped" and "provided." That narrows the potential choices to A, B or C, with C being the simplest, most direct, and grammatically correct sentence.

Question: 7
Answer: C

If you start a sentence with "finding the Baltimore waterfront fascinating," the next word has to be "Antonio" as he is the one being referred to.

Question: 8
Answer: A

This word "with" brings us into the present tense, making choice A the only possible answer as all of the other choices are in the past tense.

Question: 9
Answer: D

We have to choose an answer here that:

1) makes it clear that the bats, not the people, eat the insects
2) is written in a simple, straightforward manner

Question: 10
Answer: A

Choice A is the simplest, most direct, way of wording the sentence and the only one that is grammatically correct.

Question: 11
Answer: A

The correct answer here is the one with parallel sentence structure; "the enforcement"… and "the education"…..are parallel.

Question: 12
Answer: B

To identify the correct pronoun in a sentence, eliminate the other people and see which one works. Would you say, "me was so startled" or "I was so startled"?

Question: 13
Answer: D

The word "writes" must be replaced with the word "wrote" as we are talking about the past.

Question: 14
Answer: C
The entire sentence must be in the same tense. He "saw himself"….. so he "believed"…..

Question: 15
Answer: B

Whenever there is the word "neither" in a sentence, you have to have the word "nor." Whenever there is the word "either" in a sentence, you have to have the word "or." Remember the rule, "either/or, neither/nor."

Question: 16
Answer: C

We have to replace "has been" with "was" since we are talking about the past.

Question: 17
Answer: D

Look at the end of the sentence where it was "workers are essentially a slave laborer." The word "workers" is plural, so we have to end with the words "slave laborers."

Question: 18
Answer: C

We have to replace the word "they" with "it" since we are referring to the proposed tax.

Question: 19
Answer: E

There is no grammatical error here, so the answer is "E"

Question: 20
Answer: B

In order for the subject and the verb to agree, we have to say the managers "hold us" responsible.

Question: 21
Answer: C

Look at the end of the sentence. For parallel sentence structure, we have to say "the combination of strength and agility."

Question: 22
Answer: D

We have to change the word "are "to "is" because it has to agree with the word "obsession."

Question: 23
Answer: A

We have to change the phrase "arrived to" to "arrived in" since we don't arrive to a place.

Question: 24
Answer: E

There are no grammatical errors here, making the correct choice "E"

Question: 25
Answer: C

We have to change the word "continues" to "continue" since it agrees with the word "flights."

Question: 26
Answer: D

The grammatically correct wording would be "offers of assistance" not "offers for assistance."

Question: 27
Answer: E

This sentence is grammatically correct, so the answer is "E."

Question: 28
Answer: C

This sentence is ambiguous....which means that it is vague or unclear. Since two women are named, Ms. Perez and Ms. Tanaka, we do not know which one is being referred to when it says "her" son.

Question: 29
Answer: E

This sentence is grammatically correct, so the answer is "E."

Question: 30
Answer: E

Choice E simply states who "purists" are.

Question: 31
Answer: C

The word "ones" in sentence 3 refers to the "reviews" in sentence 2.

Question: 32
Answer: C

The previous sentences are referring to Romeo and Juliet. So the best transition would be "Another supposed outrage...."

Question: 33
Answer: A

The first sentence of the first paragraph (and its supporting sentences) take an opposite point of view from the first sentence of the second paragraph (and its supporting sentences).

Question: 34
Answer: E

Choice E is the only option that makes this sentence grammatically correct.

Question: 35
Answer: B

Since the focus in this sentence is changing to Austen from Shakespeare, it should be worded, "Austen, too, would see...."

Test 2

Section 7: Critical Reading

Question: 1
Answer: D

> Vocabulary:
> A) ensured (guaranteed)
> B) approved (agreed to)
> C) belittled (made something, or someone, seem unimportant)
> D) **eliminated (completely removed)**
> E) defended (protected from danger)

Any possibility of Geoffrey being reelected was completely removed, or "eliminated."

Question: 2
Answer: C

> Vocabulary:
> A) amateurish (unskillful) professional (skillful)
> B) lax (slipshod, negligent) harsh (unpleasantly rough)

C) **selective (choose carefully) inclusive (everything included)**
D) judgmental (excessively critical) discriminating (showing good judgment)
E) sensitive (delicate, easily damaged) insightful (perceptive, intuitive)

The word "although" tells you there will be a contrast. The "uneven quality" lets you know that the editors were including a poor quality of material, mixed in with that of good quality, so they were being "inclusive." Their reputation of being "selective" does, indeed, contrast with being "inclusive."

Question: 3
Answer: D

   Vocabulary:
   A) verbose (wordy, long-winded) mundane (common, ordinary)
   B) concise (brief, to the point)......elaborate (complicated, detailed)
   C) comprehensive (understandable)......edifying (educational, instructive)
   D) **succinct (brief, concise)......enlightening (informative, instructive)**
   E) provocative (provoking, annoying)......technical (relating to a particular subject)

The first word refers to "brief" and the second refers to "instructive." So choices B and D work for the first blank, and choices C and D work for the second blank. Therefore, choice B is the only one that works for both.

Question: 4
Answer: E

   Vocabulary:
   A) An aggregation (collection from various sources)

B) An inclination (tendency)
C) A prognosis (prediction)
D) A retrenchment (cutback)
E) A preeminence (prestige, prominence)

We need to choose a word that means "a popularity." The only one that works is "preeminence."

Question: 5
Answer: A

Vocabulary:
A) unequivocal (unmistakable, clear)
B) effusive (unrestrained, lavish)
C) incorrigible (incurable, hopeless)
D) tenuous (weak, fragile, unconvincing)
E) Ineffable (unable to be expressed in words)

We need a word that means clear-cut or unmistakable, making the correct answer choice A.

Question: 6
Answer: D

The first sentence of the passage gives the definition of a "movement." It says, "a movement is......." making the correct answer choice D.

Question: 7
Answer: B

The last sentence says that Black writers and artists....."sought to transform" the ways Black Americans "were represented or portrayed in literature and the arts." Since "transform" means "to alter" and "represented or portrayed" means "depicted," the sentence is saying the exact same thing as choice B.

Question: 8
Answer: C

This passage explains that the term "cool" has stayed in use much longer than most other slang words. Therefore, it is noting the durability (or endurance) of the term "cool."

Question: 9
Answer: B

Lines 10 to 11 compare slang terms to fashion designs, saying that neither stays in style for long. In other words, they are both "ephemeral," which means short-lived or fleeting.

Question: 10
Answer: E

This passage is all about Venus, and our attempts to understand it. Therefore, the correct answer is E since an "astronomical enigma" is something perplexing relating to the planets – in this case, Venus.

Question: 11
Answer: A

In lines 11 – 14 we are told why something we might logically conclude (that Venus and Earth have a similar atmosphere) is not true. Therefore, it dismisses a "plausible supposition," which means a logical conclusion.

Question: 12
Answer: E

The first sentence of the third paragraph states that opinions vary. The next sentence starts with, "According to one theory....." Two sentences later it states, "Another intriguing theory....." Therefore the paragraph offers two different theories about Venus.

Question: 13
Answer: B

It could not be true that the atmosphere is pure carbon dioxide because, if that were the case, the vegetation and primitive life forms would not be able to survive.

Question: 14
Answer: B

In lines 32 to 34 it states that the Mariner 2 "gave us our first reliable information." That implies that previous information was not reliable or trustworthy.

Question: 15
Answer: D

The statement, "The answer can only lie…." is decisive (which means conclusive or final) because it lets us know that it is the only possible answer.

Question: 16
Answer: C

The word "regular" in the sentence is followed by the word "two-dimensionality," giving the impression that it goes on forever without change. So the best choice of a word to replace "regular" would be "unvarying."

Question: 17
Answer: B

Reading lines 4 to 8, we note that "raindrops pounded," "glistening sparks" bounced and "ephemeral jewels" disappeared into the darkness. These are certainly examples of vivid imagery.

Question: 18
Answer: E

Mami and Tata teased the author that she was "disillusioned because the streets were not paved with gold." If that's what she expected, then she certainly "harbored unrealistic expectations."

Question: 19
Answer: B

In the second paragraph, the narrator gives a very negative description of Brooklyn. So eliminate any answer where even one of the two words does not work. The narrator does not describe Brooklyn as mysterious or appealing, or multifaceted or alluring. Therefore the only answer that works is "uniform and oppressive."

Question: 20
Answer: E

The narrator and the girl kept checking each other out in a hesitant, but not a suspicious, manner. The answer that best describes this is choice E.

Question: 21
Answer: D

The discussion between the narrator and the girl focuses on what it means to be "Hispanic," which is an ethnic label.

Question: 22
Answer: B

The narrator says, "I'd always been Puerto Rican, and it hadn't occurred to me that in Brooklyn I'd be someone else." She is clearly fearing the loss of her previous identity.

Question: 23
Answer: E

The mother tells the narrator that she can't just go outside to play without permission......"This isn't Puerto Rico.......Something could happen to you."
The mother is saying that there are different rules now that they are living in Brooklyn.

Question: 24
Answer: D

In the last paragraph the narrator said she "quaked" (shook with fear) and imagined that "greater dangers lay ahead." She is experiencing fear and uncertainty.

Test 2

Section 8: Math

Question: 1
Answer: B

Turn this into a fraction. 15 minutes out of 90 minutes can be written 15/90 which is reduced to 1/6.

Question: 2
Answer: D

In triangle HJK, we are told that angle JHK in a right angle. Therefore, its opposite side, JK, is the hypotenuse of the right triangle. The hypotenuse is always the longest side. (Remember the rule that the longest side of a triangle is always opposite the largest angle.)

Question: 3
Answer: C

In a linear function the difference between terms is constant. Notice that each term of f(n) increases by 6. It starts with 7, 13 and 19, so the next term has to be (19 + 6) 25. It then continues with 31 and 37.

Question: 4
Answer: C

Maly has built houses for "n" years.
Charlie has built houses for 5 years less than twice Maly.
Twice May would be "2n"
Five years less than that would be "2n − 5"

Question: 5
Answer: B

Since AD is a straight line, all of the angles forming it must total 180 degrees. Angle APB is 80 degrees. So the sum of angle BPC and angle CPD must total 100 degrees. We are told that PC is a bisector, which means that it divides angle BPD into two equal parts. Since the two angles total 100 degrees and are equal to each other, they are each 50 degrees (1/2 of 100 degrees).

Question: 6
Answer: C

If you list odd integers, you are counting by two. (e.g. 1,3,5,7, etc.) So if x is an odd integer, the next odd integer would be two greater, or x + 2.

Question: 7
Answer: A

The x coordinate of Point T is going to be negative the x coordinate of Point P (or −a).

The y coordinate of Point T is going to be the same as the y coordinate of Point P (or b)
So the correct answer is (-a, b) or choice A.

Question: 8
Answer: A

We are given all of the information that we need, but in a mixed up order.
1) The last sentence says there are 12 red glass beads.
2) The third sentence says there are 3 times as many red glass beads as   blue glass beads. Since 12/3 = 4 we know there are 4 blue glass beads.
3) The second sentence says the number of glass beads is 4 times the number of wood beads. Since there is a total of 16 glass beads (12 red + 4 blue) we can do 16/4 to find there are 4 wood beads.
The total number of beads in the box is 12 + 4 + 4 = 20

Question: 9
Answer: A

They are asking what the graph would look like if it were to be flipped across the x axis. Since choice A is the mirror image of the given graph, it is the correct answer.

Question: 10
Answer: C

If you FOIL each binomial, you will get:
$(x+y)^2 = x^2+2xy+y^2 = 100$
$(x-y)^2 = x^2-2xy+y^2 = 16$
If we subtract the second equation from the first we get:
$4xy = 84$
Divide both sides by 4 and find:
$xy = 21$

Question: 11

Answer: A

We need to solve the inequality for x.
Add 5 to both sides to get:
4 is less than or equal to 4x
Divide both sides by 4 to get:
1 is less than or equal to x.
That is the same thing as saying that x is greater than or equal to 1. That is depicted by graph A.

Question: 12
Answer: E

Look at either of the rectangles inscribed inside the circle.
You can rotate it any number of degrees, and it would still fit inside the circle. So there are a limitless number of rectangles (much more than 4!) that can be inscribed in the circle.

Question: 13
Answer: B

The easiest way to solve this problem is to give n a value.
For example, let n = 2
Then $2^n = 4$ and $2^{n+1} = 2^3 = 8$
$4 + 8 = 12$ so K = 12
Now, the question asks what is 2^{n+2} in terms of k
If n = 2, then $2^{n+2} = 2^4 = 16$.
What is 16 in terms of k, which means what is 16 in terms of 12?
The answer is 4k/3 because 16 = 4(12)/3

Question: 14
Answer: E

Remember the rule that the longer the side, the larger the opposite angle.
So if AB is greater than AC,

then the angle opposite AB (which is z) is greater than the angle opposite AC (which is y)
So if z is greater than y, then y cannot = z making choice E false.

Question: 15
Answer: D

According to the circle graph, Tom spent 20% of his trip expenses on his hotel room. Since the total of his trip expenses was $240, he spent $48 on his hotel room ($.20 \times $240)
Note that he shared the cost of the room equally with three OTHER people. So four people were each paying $48, making the total cost of the hotel room $192 ($48 x 4)

Question: 16
Answer: E

Since the game board is in the shape of a square, the number of squares on each side of the game board must be equal. So "k," the total number of squares along all four sides of the game board, must be a multiple of 4. Look at the answer choices, and 52 (choice E) is the only one that is a multiple of 4.

Test 2

Section 9: Critical Reading

Question: 1
Answer: C

  Vocabulary:
  A) lush (luxurious, plush)
  B) sprawling (extensive, rambling)
  C) desolate (isolated, deserted)
  D) gaudy (flashy, showy, flamboyant)

E) monumental (massive, enormous)

The clue words in the sentence are "isolation and loneliness." Those feelings would reflect a desolate landscape.

Question: 2
Answer: B

Vocabulary:
A) misnomer (contradiction, inaccuracy)
B) hybrid (crossbreed)
C) vector (path, trajectory)
D) curative (healing, therapeutic)
E) precursor (forerunner, predecessor)

The portion of the sentence after the blank gives the definition of a hybrid plant.

Question: 3
Answer: A

Vocabulary:
A) Stringent (strict, rigorous)
B) Dispersive (scattering, separating)
C) Conditional (dependent on something else being done)
D) Recessive (receding)
E) Obtrusive (conspicuous, prominent)

If the testing was rigorous, than it was "stringent," which is a synonym for the word rigorous.

Question: 4
Answer: D

Vocabulary:
A) revolutionary (groundbreaking) promoted (endorsed, sponsored)

B) positive (optimistic, confident) prohibited (forbidden, banned)
C) successful (positive, effective) protested (objected, opposed)
D) **divisive (conflict-ridden) restricted (limited, constrained)**
E) militant (combative, confrontational) fostered (nurtured)

Let's look at the second blank first. We want it to mean forbidden or limited, which narrows down the possible answers to B and D. Now, for the first blank, we want a word with a negative connotation. Therefore, "divisive" works, but "positive" does not.

Question: 5
Answer: A

Vocabulary:
A) **Bucolic (rural, relating to the countryside or country life)**
B) Prolific (productive, creative, fruitful)
C) Lugubrious (sad, mournful, gloomy)
D) Sundry (various, miscellaneous, assorted)
E) Metaphorical (figurative, symbolic)

This is a vocabulary question. The portion of the sentence after the blank defines the word "bucolic."

Question: 6
Answer: E

Vocabulary:
A) Misguided (ill-advised, mistaken)........remonstrance (evidence, proof)
B) Absurd (ridiculous, illogical)........erudition (knowledge, education)
C) Plausible (believable, reasonable)........lassitude (weariness, tiredness)

D) Painstaking (thorough, meticulous)……..fabrication (creation, untruth)
E) **Wrongheaded (foolish, unwise)………chicanery (deception, trickery)**

Consider each blank separately. For the first blank, we need a word that means ill-advised or foolish, narrowing the choices to A or E. For the second blank, we need a word that means deception because "skewed data" is information or statistics that are distorted or biased. This limits the correct answer to E.

Question: 7
Answer: C

Both authors agree that comic books have no have no educational value. The author of Passage 1 actually accuses them of being "anti-educational." The author of Passage 2 refers to them as "junk," but says they're a good outlet for kids when they are stressed.

Question: 8
Answer: A

Read the complete sentence that begins in line 3, and determine which word you can substitute for "question" and still retain the original meaning of the sentence. The only word that works is "matter."

Question: 9
Answer: C

The author explains in the very next sentence (lines 13 to 15) that learning and entertainment occur simultaneously.

Question: 10
Answer: D

The three sentences in lines 18 to 22 all start with the words, "They do not...." and elaborate on things children do not learn from reading comic books. The children are therefore being "shortchanged," which means to be given less than they deserve.

Question: 11
Answer: E

In the first paragraph of Passage 2 the author refutes lines 24 to 27 of Passage 1 by saying that there are adult comic book fans in many walks of life who continue to buy and save comic books.

Question: 12
Answer: C

In lines 70 to 80 it describes the many pressures exerted on children, and explains that they need a form of escape, a "relief zone," which in the author's day was achieved through the reading of comic books.

Question: 13
Answer: B

Quotation marks are used around the word "fanzines" to identify an unusual, but very specific, term.

Question: 14
Answer: D

The author of Passage 2 states emphatically that comic books are junk. He considers attempts to portray them as "educational junk" to be a failure because he says there is no such thing.

Question: 15
Answer: E

In line 57 the word "compromised" immediately follows the word "basest," which means worthless or of low morals. We are therefore looking for a negative word, and "degraded" fits perfectly in the context of the sentence.

Question: 16
Answer: D

The author, in lines 68 to 87, explains that children have very stressful lives (not even getting a coffee break!) and need a form of escape (comic books) through which they can recharge their batteries before resuming their pressured lives.

Question: 17
Answer: E

Passage 1 concludes with the statement that comic books "suggest many things that are harmful." The author of Passage 1 would therefore use the information in lines 81 to 83 as further support of this premise.

Question: 18
Answer: C

The tone of Passage 1 is definitely "severe," which means harsh. The author not only believes that comic books have no educational value, the author believes they are "anti-educational!" That is definitely harsh, or "severe."

Test 2

Section 10: Writing

Question: 1
Answer: B

Remember that the verbs must agree. They "practiced" so they "would know."

Question: 2
Answer: C

Putting all of the information in chronological order, as is done in choice "C," is the simplest, most direct way of wording this sentence.

Question: 3
Answer: C

This sentence takes place in the past tense. Although women....."voted," suffrage...."was not established."

Question: 4
Answer: B

In order for everything to agree, this sentence should be worded, "Bees must leave.....at the risk........"

Question: 5
Answer: E

Tie the end of the sentence back to the beginning. "It took the Museum.......to acquire......."

Question: 6
Answer: E

The simplest, most straightforward way of wording this sentence is clearly choice "E."

Question: 7
Answer: A

The underlined portion of the sentence is correct the way it is written with "should" and "would" in the same tense.

Question: 8
Answer: D

We need parallel sentence structure, so the grammatically correct wording would be "considerable ability in math and in foreign languages."

Question: 9
Answer: A

The sentence, as it is written, is the simplest, most direct way of wording the information and clearly has parallel sentence structure.

Question: 10
Answer: B

The correct way of wording this sentence would state, "many Szechuan recipes require that…." This narrows down the possible choices to (B) and (D). Since this is a cause and effect sentence, it is best to start the sentence with the word "because."

Question: 11
Answer: D

We have to compare the music of Gershwin to the music of his contemporaries, not to the other composers themselves.

Question: 12
Answer: E

Using the word "thus" is the simplest way of connecting the information in the beginning of the sentence with the information at the end of the sentence.

Question: 13
Answer: A

The first word of the underlined portion of the sentence must state who "indicated their desire to extend free enterprise." It is clearly "Canadians," making choice (A) the only possible answer.

Question: 14
Answer: C

We are talking about researchers in this sentence. They "praise studies" and they "rarely show kindness," making choice (C) the best option.

300 WORDS FREQUENTLY
SEEN ON THE SAT

(Learn 10 words per day and be ready in a month!)

abstemious – self-disciplined, moderate
accord – agreement, concurrence
acumen – shrewdness, insight, good judgment
adamant – stubborn, inflexible, obstinate
adept – skillful, adroit
adequate – enough, acceptable, sufficient
aesthetic – pertaining to beauty or the arts
affable – friendly, easy-going
alacrity – promptness in response, eagerness, readiness
amalgam – mixture, combination
ambiguous – vague, unclear
ambivalent – unsure, undecided
ameliorate – improve, upgrade
amiable – friendly, agreeable
anachronistic – out-dated
analogous – comparable, similar
analogy – comparison, equivalence
anecdote – a short narrative or amusing story
animosity – hostility, feeling of resentment
apathy – lack of feeling or emotion, indifference
apocryphal – untrue, made up
appropriate – suitable, proper
articulate – express clearly in words
ascetic – one who denounces worldly pleasures and desires
assiduous – hard-working, diligent
astute – shrewd, clever, perceptive
atypical – not typical, uncharacteristic
audacious – bold, daring
augment – increase, expand, supplement
auspicious – promising, suggesting future success is likely
authenticity – quality of being genuine, legitimate or valid
autonomy – independence, self-sufficiency
avarice – greed

banal – commonplace, ordinary
banter – playful conversation
belligerent – hostile, inclined to fight
beneficiary – recipient, receiver
benevolent – kind, caring, compassionate
benign – of gentle disposition, non-threatening
bifurcation – divergence, branching, split
blatant – obvious, unconcealed

cacophonous – harsh sounding, discordant, unmelodious
callousness – insensitivity, heartlessness
cantankerous – irritable, crabby, argumentative
capricious – unpredictable, changeable
catalyst – something that causes change
catastrophic – disastrous, devastating
cathartic – therapeutic, healing, liberating
cavil – make frivolous objections, quibble
charlatan – an imposter, quack
circumspect – cautious, careful, prudent
clairvoyant – able to predict the future
clemency – leniency or pardon
cloistered – sheltered, confined, secluded
cloying – distasteful by reason of excess, overly sentimental
cogent – convincing, forceful, persuasive
collaborative – cooperative, working together
compensation – payment, reward
complacent – satisfied, content
compunction – regret, reluctance, second thoughts
conciliatory – overcoming distrust or hostility
concord – agreement, harmony
condescending – acting in a superior manner, patronizing
conflagration – big fire
conformist – person who follows accepted rules and customs
conjecture – guess, estimation, speculation
connoisseur – specialist, expert, authority
consecrated – holy, sacred, sanctified
contempt – dislike, disdain, hatred
contiguous – touching, neighboring

contrite – remorseful, sorrowful
convergence – coming together, joining of separate elements
convivial – pleasant, welcoming, hospitable
cornucopia – state of abundance
credulity – naivete, gullibility
cursory – superficial, brief, passing
cynical – skeptical, suspicious

defiant – disobedient, rebellious
deleterious – harmful, destructive
demean – humiliate, degrade
depicted – portrayed, represented
desecrate – to destroy the sanctity or holiness
despondent – sad, unhappy, discouraged
diaphanous – transparent, delicate
diatribe – verbal attack, rant
diffident – shy, insecure, timid
digress – go off topic, deviate
dilatory – slow, causing delay
diminutive – small in size, miniscule
disconcerted – taken aback, confused, unsettled
disdainful – scornful, contemptuous
disheartened – discouraged, depressed, saddened
disparage – ridicule, belittle
disseminate – distribute, spread
dissension – disagreement, opposition
divergent – separating, moving in different directions
dogmatic – dictatorial, rigid, inflexible
dubious – doubtful, uncertain
dupe – deceive or trick

ebullient – cheerful, jovial, enthusiastic
eclectic – selected from various sources
edified – informed, educated, enlightened
efficacious – effective
elegy – poem or song expressing grief
elude – avoid, escape
embellish – decorate, make fancy

endowment – donation, gift
empathic – feeling the sufferings of others
endowment – donation
enigma – paradox, conundrum
ephemeral – short-lived, transient, fleeting
equitable – fair, just, reasonable
equivocal – vague, ambiguous, unclear
erratic – unpredictable, inconsistent
erroneous – wrong, incorrect, mistaken
erudite – scholarly, knowledgeable, well-educated
esoteric – hard to understand
exacerbate – make worse, aggravate
exemplar – example, model
exhilarated – overjoyed, delighted, elated
extol – to praise, exalt
extrapolate – infer, draw conclusions
extricate – untangle, disengage

facilitate – help, assist, ease
fastidious – demanding, finicky, painstaking
feasible – possible, achievable, reasonable
feign –pretend
fetid – stinking, having an offensive odor
fetter – a chain or shackle, restrict motion
fidelity – loyalty, faithfulness
filial – relating to one's family
flaw – error, imperfection, defect
flippant – frivolous, not serious
flourish – embellishment, decoration
fortuitous – happening by chance with good results, fortunate
fractious – quarrelsome, unruly, rebellious
fragility – delicateness, breakability
fundamental – basic, central, important
futility – uselessness, pointlessness

gaiety – cheerfulness, joy
garish – gaudy, showy, brash
garrulous – talkative, verbose

hedonist – person whose objective is one's own pleasure
highlight – high point, best part
homogeneous – of uniform composition

iconoclast – radical, revolutionary, free thinker
idealist – a perfectionist, romantic
immutable – unchangeable
impassive – giving no sign of feeling or emotion
impeccable – perfect, without flaw
impervious – not allowing entrance or passage
impetuous – acting in a rash manner without thinking
impulsive – spontaneous, unwary, thoughtless
incendiary – flammable, provocative
incipient – beginning, in an early stage
incongruous – incompatible, inconsistent, inharmonious
inconsequential – of little importance
incredulous – disbelieving, skeptical, doubtful
indigent – suffering from extreme poverty
indolent – habitually lazy, idle
industrious – hardworking, diligent
inept – incompetent, unskilled
innate – existing within, inherent
innocuous – harmless
insatiable – greedy, incapable of being satisfied
inscrutable – mysterious, hard to understand
insincere – not sincere, two-faced, disingenuous
insolent – rude, disrespectful
integrity – honesty, truth
intransigence – stubbornness, refusal to compromise
intrepid – brave, fearless, adventurous
intricacy - complexity
inundate – overwhelm, flood
invaluable – extremely valuable, priceless
irony – paradox, satire, double meaning
irresolute – indecisive, wavering, vacillating
itinerant – wandering from place to place, nomadic

juxtapose – place side by side
jubilant- ecstatic, thrilled, delighted

laconic – brief, concise, terse
lament – verbally express grief
languid – sluggish, without energy
laud – praise, speak well of
liability – responsibility, obligation, burden
liberality – open-mindedness, tolerance, progressiveness
loquacious – talkative, verbose
lugubrious – sad, mournful, somber, morose

machinations – conspiracies, collusions, plotting
malign – speak evil of
mandate – an order, command, directive
maverick – unconventional person, nonconformist, one of a kind
mediate – negotiate, arbitrate, act as a go-between
mercenary – greedy, moneygrubbing; a soldier
mercurial – changeable, unpredictable
metaphor – symbol, representation
miniscule – very small
mitigate – lessen, alleviate
mollified – calmed, appeased, placated
moribund – on the way out, dying, declining
morose – depressed, gloomy, sullen
mundane – ordinary, commonplace
myopic – narrow-minded, prejudiced, intolerant

naïve - simple, childlike, unexperienced
nebulous – unclear, vague
neophyte – beginner, amateur
novice – beginner

obliterate – wipe out, destroy, demolish
obscure – unclear, vague
optimistic – having a positive outlook
opulent – luxurious, lavish, sumptuous

ornate – decorative, over-elaborate
orthodox – conventional, accepted, traditional
ostentatious – showy, displaying wealth

paradox – inconsistency, contradiction
pathological – compulsive, extreme, uncontrolled
paucity – scarcity, lack
pensive – thoughtful, reflective
peremptory – dictatorial, authoritative, decisive
perfidious – disloyal, dishonest, treacherous
permeate – spread throughout
pessimistic – having a negative outlook, cynical
petulant – sulky, moody, grumpy
phlegmatic – calm in temperament, sluggish
placate – to appease, pacify, soothe or mollify
platitude – cliché, commonplace expression
plethora – overabundance, surfeit
pompous – arrogant, self-important
pragmatic - practical
precipitate – to cause to happen
precipitous – impulsive, rash, quick, hasty
predictable – expected, anticipated
primacy – importance, priority
prodigal – wasteful, extravagant
proficiency – skill, expertise
propensity – tendency, inclination
propitiate – appease, placate, calm down
prosaic – commonplace, ordinary, dull
provincial – narrow-minded, unsophisticated
puerile – childish, immature

querulous – irritable, complaining
quiescent – inactive, still
quixotic – idealistic

rancorous – bitter, malicious, vindictive, spiteful
refute – to prove wrong
remuneration – payment, salary, wage

resolute – determined, firm, unyielding
respite – a period of rest or relief
reticent – reserved, discreet, not forthcoming
reverent – respectful, worshipful

sagacity - wisdom
salutary – helpful, beneficial
sanctimonious – pompous, self-righteous, smug
sanctity – holiness, sacredness
scrutinize – inspect, study carefully
sedulous – zealous, hardworking, conscientious
solicitous – considerate, caring
somber – gloomy, melancholy, depressed
spurious – unauthentic, false, fake
startling – surprising, amazing
submissive – passive, meek, obedient
substantiate – validate, confirm, prove to be true
subtle – understated, hard to detect
succulent – mouthwatering, luscious
supercilious – arrogant, condescending, superior
superficial – concerned only with the obvious, shallow
superfluous – extra, unnecessary, excessive
supplant – replace or substitute
surmount – overcome, prevail
surreptitious – secret, sneaky
sycophant – flatterer, brown-noser
syncopated – modified, cut short, abbreviated

tacit – implied, unspoken
temporize – delay, put off, procrastinate
tenable – reasonable, acceptable, rational
tenacious – stubborn, obstinate
terse – concise,
thespian – an actor or actress
totalitarian – dictatorial, tyrannical
transience – briefness, brevity
trenchant – keen, sharp, incisive
truculent – hostile, belligerent, defiant

ubiquitous – existing everywhere at the same time
unruffled – not bothered, calm, tranquil

vacillate – to waver, act in an indecisive manner
vehement – passionate, powerful, fervent
venerable – respected, esteemed
verbose – wordy
versatile – adaptable, multipurpose
vexing – annoying, displeasing
vindicate – exonerate, release from blame or suspicion
vindictive – disposed to seek revenge, spiteful
virtuoso – one skilled in the fine arts
vitriolic – spiteful, hurtful
vituperative - insulting, abusive, offensive
voluminous – marked by great volume or bulk

wavering –indecisive, uncertain
wistful – reflective, thoughtful, contemplative

zealot – an extremist or fanatic individual

30766982R00070

Made in the USA
Charleston, SC
26 June 2014